Hardy Ferns

Hardy
Ferns

Michael
Jefferson-Brown

WARD LOCK

First published in Great Britain in 1992
by Ward Lock Limited, Villiers House, 41/47 Strand,
London WC2N 5JE, England

A Cassell Imprint

Text filmset
by Chapterhouse, The Cloisters, Formby L37 3PX

Printed and bound in Spain
by Graficas Reunidas, Madrid

British Library Cataloguing in Publication Data. A catalogue
record for this book is available from the British Library.

ISBN 0–7063–7069–4

**Moisture-loving neighbours with the soft shield
fern, *Polystichum setiferum*, including hostas,
arums and *Rheum palmatum*.**

Contents

Preface

With the increased interest in the use of foliage in garden design, it is hardly surprising that the popularity of ferns has also taken an upswing. Ferns themselves are so wonderfully designed that they cannot fail to make an atmospheric impact in any garden.

Perhaps because ferns are somehow considered 'different' from other garden plants, they are approached a little warily and even keen gardeners have often not ventured to plant more than the familiar hart's tongue or male fern. Yet the range is huge – from tiny wall-clinging varieties to imposing tree-like specimens – and the aim of this book is to introduce as wide a range as possible of the hardy varieties of this fascinating family.

It is pleasant to write about plants that are easy to grow provided a few simple guidelines are followed. Nor is the cost going to deter anyone; healthy young plants can be bought at very reasonable prices. Small, pot-grown specimens soon get established, often more quickly than larger plants. Ferns are for everyone. Building a collection can be a fascinating pastime and some of the more unusual kinds can be exchanged with fellow enthusiasts.

There is plenty of practical advice on the care and propagation of ferns, and on how to create a fernery, but most of all I hope the ideas for using ferns alongside other plants and for incorporating some of the more unusual and interesting varieties into the overall garden design will provide inspiration and encouragement – and even win some more converts to pteridology!

Fern border with witch hazel to rear. In semi-shade are hart's tongue (*Asplenium scolopendrium*), male fern form (*Dryopteris filix-mas*) and lady fern (*Athyrium filix-femina).*

CHAPTER 1

Introducing Ferns

Ferns are among the world's oldest living things, they dominated the planet's vegetation through the Carboniferous period, well over 200 million years ago, when they would have been growing with huge mosses and horsetails that could have been thirty metres – a hundred feet high!

Ferns remain an important part of our vegetation. Their diversity and intricate designs have given botanists lots of scope for debate; they generally agree that there are around 10,500 species arranged in some 240 genera. Little wonder there are several views of their botanical arrangement. While there are some exceptional annual species, most are long-lived perennials that have their roots well dug into the soil. A few send slender scrambling stems up trees or rocks to become climbers. Quite a number grow as epiphytes, plants perching on trees and rooting into the plant debris lodged in nooks on the branches, but these are more numerous in humid tropical forests. Others are adapted to life on rockfaces; there are a handful of attractive small species such as wall rue and the rusty-back fern that were originally rock-dwellers but have jumped gratefully on to man-made walls, often forming considerable colonies.

Sizes range from the wall rue, *Asplenium ruta-muraria*, which usually only reaches a height of about 5–6 cm (2–3 in), to the tree ferns found in New Zealand and elsewhere, the largest of which can have trunks over 10 m (30 ft) high. The size of ferns in a cool temperate climate varies hugely according to their habitat. The widespread male ferns, *Dryopteris filix-mas*, may be scarcely 60 cm (2 ft) in one site but up to 1.5 m (5 ft) in another. Fronds of the royal fern, *Osmunda regalis*, are capable of growing as long as 3.5 m (12 ft) in an ideal habitat, though in less wet and luxuriant places they may measure only 60 cm (2 ft).

Habits of growth

Many ferns are definitely deciduous, the fronds rusting and collapsing with the frosts of autumn. Hillsides of bracken, *Pteidium aquilinum*, turn from the fresh green of unfurling fronds to the rich mature colour of summer and then to the golds and fawn buffs of autumn followed by deeper rusty shades. Some ferns try for evergreen status and will make it in milder winters, though fading and becoming sensibly deciduous in harder times; other species are steadfastly evergreen.

The leaf surfaces, the fronds, may be uncut, botanically 'entire', like the hart's tongue fern, *Asplenium scolopendrium*, that can carpet the ground of moist woods and copses, or can be so intricately cut as to rival filigree lacework.

While all species increase from dust-like spores released from the fruiting organs located on the underside of adult fronds, a number of kinds augment this method by sending out stoloniferous shoots below ground, each of which will start a new plant. Others will produce small plantlets on some of the fronds, with these either rooting if in contact with the soil and then becoming independent, or, when mature, dropping away from the frond and then rooting into the soil to start a new plant.

Ferns are widely distributed throughout the world. Some remain almost identical throughout their distribution, but others are more volatile and will mutate to produce many variations, some remarkably dissimilar to the parent species. The soft shield fern, *Polystichum setiferum*, for example, has had over 300 mutant forms named, some of these being very desirable and sought-after cultivars.

Culture in the past

The hey-day of fern culture was in the Victorian age, when it was not unusual for the whole family to set out on fern forays, digging up interesting specimens from the countryside and bringing them back to grow in their gardens. Even the most modest mutation was likely to be seized upon as a find and the specimen dug up and transported back home to be planted up outside in the fernery. Such behaviour would be regarded now as criminally vandalous, and rightly so. There are plenty of fern specialists who propagate from nursery stock, and plants are easily raised from spores collected in the wild without damaging growing plants.

The next step for the Victorians would have been to confer a name on the find. The genus and species having been determined, further descriptive Latin names were tacked on until some poor plants were saddled with names five or six words long – almost a descriptive sentence.

The inclination of some ferns to spawn mutations freely meant that at the height of the fern cult some species had over 300 cultivars listed under their specific name. There are still considerable numbers of cultivars available but the lists do not approach these phrenetic lengths. Nowadays names tend to be shorter; generic and specific names may be followed by a varietal name and if necessary by a form name, this last being in English and often being the name of the person distinguishing the form.

As pollution in the cities and towns got worse, many ferns suffered badly and enthusiasts began to grow their specimens in cool conditions under glass. Ferneries so created were a feature of many houses in Victorian times and such culture was popular till the outbreak of the First World War. At that time some of the stately gardens had very large collections both outside and under glass. The vastly changed economic conditions that emerged after the First World War caused upheavals in gardens as elsewhere. Most collections suffered and very many were either lost or very severely restricted.

Today several factors have combined to encourage a renaissance of interest in ferns. First, air pollution has been much improved; ferns, with their ability to act as monitors of bad air pollution, will now grow happily once more in areas where they have not been seen for decades. Most ferns enjoy at least some shade and as modern housing and building is getting more cramped the extra proportion of shade does provide suitable living quarters that other plants may find difficult.

However, the most important factor in this renewed interest is the realization of the beauty of these plants. They are some of the loveliest of living things. Also they seem to bring with them a sense of unusual atmosphere, perhaps something unavoidable with such age-old plants, lending a garden or a part of it a feeling of peace and timelessness almost impossible to achieve with other plants.

The garden designer must have ferns. In shade, by water, under trees, between shrubs, in the rock garden or miniature plantings ferns are invaluable.

Dryopteris filix-mas 'Grandiceps'. A crested form of the strong male fern. 'Grandiceps' is a name covering a series of plants of this type.

9

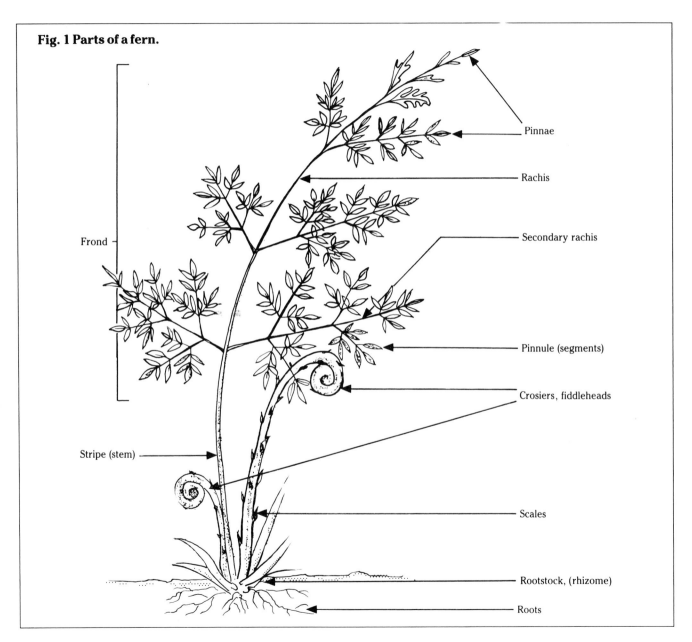

Fig. 1 Parts of a fern.

Pinnae

Rachis

Secondary rachis

Pinnule (segments)

Crosiers, fiddleheads

Frond

Stripe (stem)

Scales

Rootstock, (rhizome)

Roots

11

Fig. 2 Frond forms.

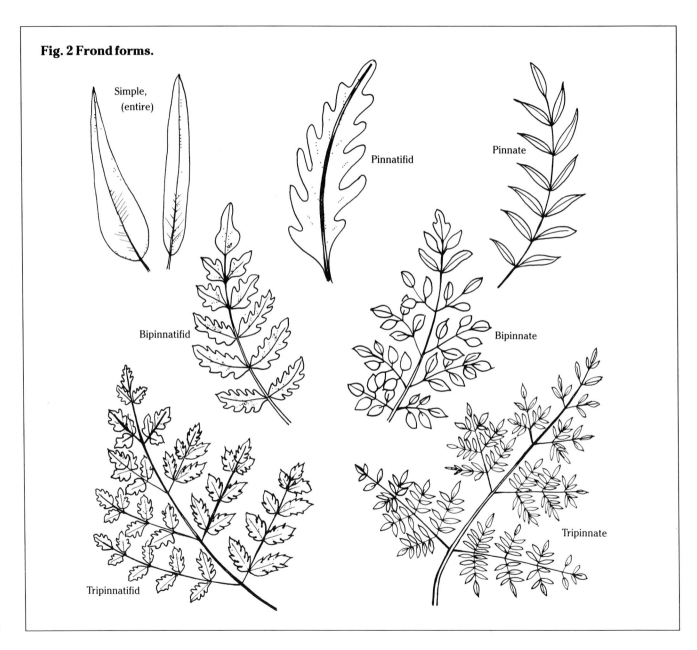

Simple, (entire)

Pinnatifid

Pinnate

Bipinnatifid

Bipinnate

Tripinnatifid

Tripinnate

Their working parts

Gardeners used to the normal run of plants can find ferns just a little strange. They organize their lives differently from most garden plants. Without loading the text with abstruse botanical terms it makes sense to describe briefly some of the parts of the plants and the way they work (Fig. 1). This can be important to make sure cultural methods are sensible.

FRONDS

These may be whole, expressed botanically as 'simple' or 'entire', like those of the hart's tongue fern, or they may be divided like those of bracken (Fig. 2). The blade of the frond can extend almost to soil level as in the lady fern or be borne aloft by a stem or stripe, as in bracken.

Fronds of a plant may all look alike whether they are sterile ones, or are fertile with spore-carrying 'sori' on the underside, but in some species such as the ostrich feather fern, (*Matteuccia struthiopteris*), sterile and fertile fronds are completely dissimilar (Fig. 3).

FROND DIVISION

Specific descriptive words are used to describe the complexity of the division of fern fronds. These sound a lot more complicated than they are, and the following can be referred to until one is certain of their meaning.

Pinnatifid Frond blade is lobed like an oak leaf, but the lobes do not reach down to the midrib (rachis).

Pinnate Frond blade is divided into segments (pinnae), the division reaching down to the rachis.

Fig. 3 Dimorphic fern, *Blechnum*, sterile and fertile fronds.

13

Familiar examples are the ash and rowan leaf.

From these the complexity increases by there being further stages in the division. Each of the first set of segments can be further divided to give twice-divided fronds:

Bipinnatifid The rachis supports a series of pinnae which are lobed but not divided down to the secondary rachis.

Bipinnate In fronds that are twice-pinnate the rachis supports a series of pinnae, each of which is divided down to the secondary rachis. These ultimate segments are called pinnules.

Further divisions take the blade division from double to three, four or even five times. Obviously the greater the division the more intricate the appearance and often the greater the beauty. Some of the most popular and pleasing of ferns have their blades three times divided: *tripinnatifid* (each of the secondary divided segments are now lobed) and *tripinnate* (the secondary segments are divided down to the tertiary rachis, giving now quite small segments or pinnules). These divisions may also be described as two, three, four etc. times pinnate.

SORI AND SPORES

Sori are the fruiting bodies found on the underside of fertile fronds. They vary in shape and arrangement, a most important diagnostic feature. The sori are made up of clusters of capsules, known as sporangia, which contain the spores by which ferns increase (Fig. 4). They act in a distinctly different way from seeds.

Grasses and ferns in a Worcestershire garden. In the foreground is a *Polystichum setiferum* form and also featured is a male fern.

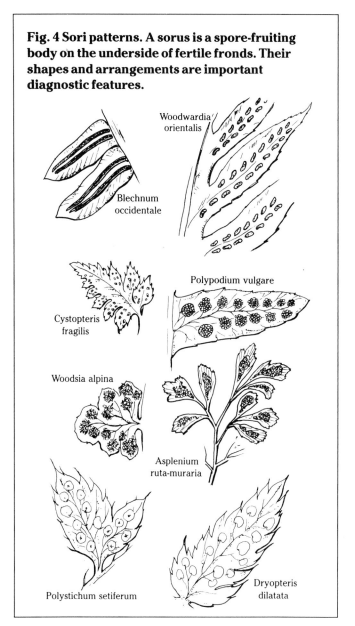

Fig. 4 Sori patterns. A sorus is a spore-fruiting body on the underside of fertile fronds. Their shapes and arrangements are important diagnostic features.

Woodwardia orientalis

Blechnum occidentale

Polypodium vulgare

Cystopteris fragilis

Woodsia alpina

Asplenium ruta-muraria

Polystichum setiferum

Dryopteris dilatata

Ferns are produced in a two-generation process. The spore, unlike a seed, has no embryo – that is, a plant-in-waiting genetically programmed from its parents. If a spore lands on a suitable surface it germinates to form a flat green cell mass called a prothallus. This has fine hair-roots holding it to the soil surface but cannot itself grow into a fern proper. The scaly flat prothallus will produce organs of two kinds, male and female. The male organ, the antheridium, releases a host of minute bodies, antherozoids, which, like animal sperm, are mobile. Tails lash these bodies through films of moisture towards the female organ, the archegonium, within the centre of which there is a free germ or egg-cell with which the antherozoids can combine and begin to produce the first small frond. At this time the first-generation part of the fern cycle, the flat prothallus, wastes away (Fig. 14).

ROOTSTOCKS

The rootstocks are the vital centres of the fern plant as they contain the growing point of the plant, the meristem. They differ in form between genera and species. Many remain as compact tufts, but others creep at soil level or just below. The extent of this creeping is from a gentle expansion of the tuft to a widespread colonizing effort. While they may all be correctly termed rhizomes, it is convenient to call the compact tufted examples rootstocks and the creeping ones rhizomes. Rhizomes may or may not branch as they expand.

Roots of ferns are fine and normally much branched. They work in the upper layers of the soil, not normally going to any great depth. Usually they react badly to their root system being disturbed.

CHAPTER 2

Ferns as Foliage Plants

In the ornamental garden ferns stand or fall as foliage plants; they have no flowers. The regal fern, *Osmunda regalis*, is sometimes called 'the flowering fern' but this is a nonsense name. It is the pinnae at the top of the upright fertile fronds densely covered with brown fruiting bodies that might just be likened to the flowering heads of an astilbe or some vigorous dock species! One has the feeling that a flowering part on a fern would be a total irrelevance, as it can be with some more orthodox plants used almost exclusively for their foliage beauty.

There are places in most gardens where it is not only possible to plant a wide selection of ferns but highly desirable because they are going to give a better return than other types of plant in the same site. Damp and shade that are anathema to many plants will suit ferns literally down to the ground. The point will not be laboured here as a chapter is devoted to the creation of a fernery, and the pros and cons together with the practical details will be explored there.

The beauty and diversity of ferns is quickly realized but is always worthy of closer attention. Aesthetically they must have a lot to contribute in most gardens. Their utility is multi-faceted and, an important point, many will grow where little else will flourish. There are types to suit most situations. There is a large number of small hardy ones whose diminutive stature and neat pleasing appearance makes them ideal companions for alpine plants, whether they be grown in a traditional rock garden, in rock beds or, indeed, in containers. Here, as elsewhere, the character of ferns is a pleasing contrast to other plants.

With the limited space of many modern gardens, every square inch has to pay the maximum rent in beauty and integrated design value. Here perhaps is the role that is waiting to be explored most popularly by the ferns. While they have a wonderful aloofness, a feeling of timelessness or almost of a parallel creation, the plants will and do associate very effectively with a wide variety of plants and may well be the first choice of companions when planting mixed beds, whether they be herbaceous, bulbous or shrubby. Needless to say, their value in light woodland is impossible to exaggerate – the raising of the ambience is dramatic. On the 'tingle factor' scale we must reach the upper levels, and the dullest person will feel the thrill.

In the herbaceous border the cool colouring, the classic design forms and their very sense of stillness makes them perfect foils to the extrovert flowering plants. The flowers are highlighted, warring colours are separated and the ferns will look tailored and distinguished when earlier herbaceous plants begin to fade away and look tired.

The habits and forms of ferns contrast completely to those of shrubs and so interact with them to provide a very dynamic picture. The varying sizes of ferns means that there are plenty to choose from, to work into the front of a shrubbery or any position further back.

The periods of the year when most ferns are at their best coincide almost exactly with the times when householders and gardeners are most likely to be out and about in the garden either working or taking their leisure. As spring warms up the majority of ferns move into more lively action and begin to unfurl new fronds, always a most exciting procedure to watch. By the end of the spring when summer weather should be arriving the ferns should be fully reclothed and looking perfect. There are small evergreen kinds that look quite reasonable through the winter – the spleenwort, *Asplenium trichomanes*, for example, which looks well either growing on a wall, in a pathway or in among small rock garden plants. However, a few months of hard weather can play havoc with some kinds that will remain pleasingly dressed and fully evergreen in milder winter and areas. The hart's tongue fern in its several forms will often look respectable and attractive in the difficult months before the late spring when glossy shining new fronds appear. These types can be planted in places more obvious in the winter months. Also outstanding as an all-weather evergreen is the common polypody, *Polypodium vulgare*, which gains its new foliage in the summer and looks fresh and lively through the winter. Particularly attractive are the forms with more intricate fronds, the cultivar *P.v.* 'Cambricum' and *P.v.* 'Cornubiense'.

Design

One works in a garden to maximize the beauty of the whole as well as of all its parts. Design is at the heart of the matter. The planting may be very naturalistic, but what may look like a happy accident is usually the result of sensitive thinking. Of course every gardener will admit that some of the happiest things that happen are really accidents. We accept the bonus with thanks and learn from them. How one tackles these matters are practical details that will be taken up in the next chapter. Here some suggested ground rules may help.

In the shade of a tall north-facing wall is *Dryopteris affinis* 'Grandiceps Askew', a distinct scaly male fern living with the contrasting *Helleborus argutifolius*.

The 'rules' are prefaced by the caveat that none of the rules are absolutes, they can be broken but their breaking is likely to be successful only when special circumstances obtain or special physical conditions have been reordered. Some of the rules may seem totally obvious, but when in haste can be overlooked.

Practical advice on preparing suitable sites, general maintenance and preferences of individual types are given in later chapters, but always bear in mind that a fern, like any other plant, should only be planted in a position where it may reasonably be expected to flourish.

Size of fern should be appropriate to the site and the companion plants. Small kinds should not be dominated by vigorous large neighbours who will inevitably force them into a subordinate position where they may eventually be swamped and killed.

The 'rule of three' states that three plants of a cultivar or a species planted in sensible proximity will be more effective than three times the effect of one plant. There is a magic factor in the equation. There may be good reasons for planting only one specimen; in limited spaces the planting of three royal ferns could be foolhardy. But where space allows, the overall design effect of three plants is, importantly, more than a collection of different singletons. Apart from the aesthetics of the matter, there is the psychological factor of a number of plants of a cultivar or species growing together suggesting that they are happy, that they have formed a colony and are increasing. The onlooker absorbs this, even if subconsciously.

Returning to visual effects, gardeners soon realize that it is a lot easier to create a pleasing design when, instead of a staccato effect of a series of single different plants, one can create varying planted shapes of plants interlocking with each other. It may well be that dissimilar larger plants and shrubs can be planted singly, their size alone helping to avoid a spotty effect.

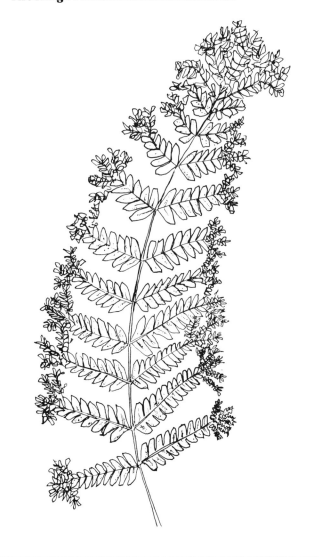

Fig. 5 Crested fern, *Dryopteris affinis* 'Cristata The King'. Pinnae and terminal crests.

Fig. 6 Cross-like doubled pinnae formation of *Athyrium filix-femina* 'Victoriae'.

But even so the background provided by drifts of plants like ferns between these shrubs or larger plants cannot help but make a more satisfying overall picture. A sense of unity is created.

The importance of contrast as a guiding principle in garden design is perhaps more relevant when the concern is with foliage and is therefore a leading consideration when planting ferns. Often the first concern of gardeners when thinking, even haphazardly, of design factors is to worry about colour. Harmony and contrast of colour is of course important, but flowers are not all, even in the herbaceous border. They come and go, but the foliage is present, if not all the time, then for a greater part of the year. It would not be wrong to start one's thinking in all garden design with foliage. This, combined with the form and habit of plants, will be the backbone of design plans.

Either planted in an area dignified with the status of a fernery or mixed with other types of plants, the ferns are going to be most effective where the individual characteristics of one kind contrast with those of another. The lacy intricacy of fronds that are three, four or five times pinnate will be enhanced by the puritan austerity of some plain dealers like the hart's tongues. The upright stance of many such as the ostrich fern against the horizontal patterns of *Polystichum setiferum* adds point and lustre to both. Another example of contrasting types that can highlight each other would be the very stylized dark-fronded *Adiantum pedatum* with upright, dark, thin stems and more or less horizontal, evenly divided frond blades and the soft shield fern or *Dryopteris erythrosorus* with their triangular paler green fronds reaching outwards from a basal rootstock.

Texture is also a factor. Some ferns are glossy highly polished artifacts, others are almost velvety. Many mutant forms have the fronds decorated with ruffled edges; others go to the extent of ending their fronds

21

with crests like some fancy type of fowl. Very ornate ones can make their fronds highly textured with ruffles and crested parts not only at the end of each frond but all down each side of them (Figs. 5 & 6). A vigorous dressy example can be cited from the many male fern mutants: *Dryopteris filix-mas* 'Grandiceps Wills' quickly makes a multi-crowned plant with fronds having neatly crested pinnae and substantial terminal crests. Quite extraordinary is the tatting fern, *Athyrium filix-femina* 'Frizelliae', with very narrow fronds having pinnae almost rolled up into little balls or beads along each side of the rachis (midrib). There are many variants of the tatting fern; in *A.f-f.* 'Frizelliae Capitatum' the terminal crests are much branched, a most unusual design.

And of course there is colour. There are many greens from pale golden greens to apple shades and dark, almost blue-greens. Some have their young foliage flushed with red, orange and bronzes, and a few will keep at least a portion of this colouring through life – one of the most popular is *Dryopteris erythrosorus* with well-cut triangular fronds a polished coppery pink when young. The colours hold until the frond becomes fully mature, by which time there are likely to be new young fronds with this attractive colouring. In other types the blade colour contrasts tellingly with the rachis stem colour: *Dryopteris wallichiana* has fresh fronds of lime green highlighted by the black rachis.

The role that ferns are called on to play in garden design will vary. They may well take on the lead part. Some of the larger ones, like the royal fern or the broad buckler fern, *Dryopteris dilatata*, are capable in the right site of producing fronds up to 1.5 m (5 ft) long and will have no difficulty in dominating the stage. They can be grandly theatrical. Others can be just as tellingly effective but manage it best by a corps de ballet triumph: the ostrich feather fern, *Matteuccia struthiopteris*, planted in a suitable spot, will quickly grow into a colony to create a wonderful ensemble.

The form of fern fronds can be highlighted by rocks or more rigid pieces of garden infrastructure such as these steps. The design contrast is always effective.

CHAPTER 3

Using Ferns in the Garden

Ferns belong to the long still early morning of the world. They are not of the hustle and bustle of modern times and the often rapidly changing régimes of twentieth-century gardens, and they are all the better for it. They can give to our plantings a sense of living timelessness and design devoid of any possible charge of egotistical self-importance – something that one can imagine of the bedding salvias, many strutting hybrid roses, the extrovert spring forsythias and the summer armies of geraniums in Ruritanian dress uniforms. I am not anti-flower; having spent almost my entire working life breeding them I could not be. But, and it is a monumental 'but', we ought to start in our garden designing by considering the leaves of the garden rather than the flowers of whatever field.

Ferns will associate well with almost all types of plant, their party manners are immaculate. Dignity and decorum are all. Never themselves in their cups, they will bring sobriety and distinction to more flamboyant extrovert neighbours. They are the garden's most diplomatic of plants. And now, having said that they will mix with all types, one can qualify this by saying that they do seem to be especially effective with certain genera and species of plants, an affinity obviously not based on blood relationships but on aesthetic ones and such practical matters as enjoying similar growing conditions (Fig. 7).

Suitable sites

WATERSIDE AND WET AREAS

Water is a magic element in garden design. To combine it with the beauty of ferns is big magic. Not all ferns will be happy with their roots in very wet soil but the royal fern is never more at home than growing by the waterside. Here is a plant in its element. If you have the space, planting *Osmunda regalis* by the side of either a formal or an informal pool can be one of the best bits of gardening you will ever do.

Osmunda regalis is a prima donna. It seems always more than life size! At all times it is an arresting plant. In spring there are no other plants so excitingly dramatic as the new stems reach up and the magnificent crosiers unfurl. Young fronds are a vivid sea green that becomes a richer deeper colour in maturity. The orange-brown young stalk becomes green, a contrast to the distinct upright fertile fronds, warm rusty brown flower-like spikes owing much of their colour to the fruiting organs. With the severer cold weather of autumn the fronds all turn colour and rust away, but even in the first half of winter the pile of dead foliage is impressive. The species and its cultivars will all be happy planted by the side of still or running water and can luxuriate in such sites so as to produce fronds which can measure over 3 m (10 ft) long and 1 m (3 ft) wide.

Fig. 7 Planting diagram, suggesting different types of planting sites.
**1. *Dryopteris filix-mas* 2. *D.f-m.*'Cristata'
3. *Matteuccia struthiopteris* 4. *Asplenium scolopendrium* 5. *A. trichomanes*
6. *A. ceterach* 7. *Adiantum pedatum*
8. *Dryopteris dilatata* 9. *Polypodium vulgare*
10. *Osmunda regalis* 11. *Athyrium filix-femina*.**

If space precludes such generous gestures, and one should remember that over the years a plant can develop several crowns so that the basic rootstock can form a very large tussock, then one should look to the buckler ferns, *Dryopteris dilatata* in particular.

The broad buckler fern, *Dryopteris dilatata*, is one of the most attractive of hardy species with much divided fronds. In the wild it is usually found close to water, perhaps by streams, by ponds, or in moist woods. It loves to run its roots through deep leaf mould. The size of the fronds depends on the age of the plant and the type of habitat. The species can be found low down or quite high up hillsides, but the higher specimens are likely to be much dwarfer and restricted in size than in the lush lowland spots. The usual 30–60 cm (1–2 ft) fronds can be four to five times longer in encouraging conditions. At this optimum size they go some way to approaching the proportions of the royal fern. It is a species that has produced several interesting forms, usually much smaller than the type but just as fond of a good watering hole.

Both the royal fern and the broad buckler fern are perhaps at their best close to water in an informal arrangement. They can be impressive in the civilization of formal surroundings but it seems a little unfair to try to have such marvellous plants tamed like tigers in a compound.

Other ferns worth considering for a moist spot include relations of the broad buckler fern. The hay-scented buckler fern, *Dryopteris aemula*, is a fine kind

Forms of the common polypody, *Polypodium vulgare*; here *P.v.* 'Cambricum' and others shown as colonizing ferns making very pleasing ground cover. To rear is a tree fern, *Dicksonia antarctica*, probably the hardiest of the tree ferns but requiring protection in hard winter weather.

with neatly cut fronds found growing wild in warm shady wooded areas, often by a stream or within the spray of a waterfall. *Thelypteris palustris* (syn. *D. thelypteris*) is commonly known as the marsh buckler fern and will flourish in really boggy peaty soils.

The influence of micro-climate is well demonstrated by the hart's tongue fern, *Asplenium scolopendrium*, which in moist spots can produce very long 'tongues'. The hart's tongue fern can colonize old wells and here, with the moisture and wind-sheltered environment the fronds can be 60 or even 90 cm (2–3 ft) long, two or three times their norm. Plants that have succeeded in growing in drier spots like walls or dry hedgerows can be very stunted and on occasion may have fronds only 8–10 cm (3–4 in) long. Again in areas of high rainfall or shaded moist woodland banks plants may have most of their fronds hanging downwards, with always a few upright ones for balance – an impressive picture. Performances in such natural sites suggest how these plants may be used in the garden. The hart's tongue is certainly one that will be delightful in a cool moist sheltered spot, but can look tired and second-rate in a dry spot where it can be battered and bruised by wind. There are a lot of welcome mutants of the type plant.

The lady fern, *Athyrium filix-femina* in its variety of delightful forms, is at its best in moister spots but does not require visible water.

The many forms of the scaly male fern, *Dryopteris affinis* (*D. pseudomas*) are among those that like a moist soil but also require good drainage to do well. *D.a.* 'Cristata The King' is one of the joys of the fern family, certainly one of the best of hardy kinds, but many of these *D. affinis* cultivars are exceptionally fine and easy types.

In this moist environment, hostas can grow hand-in-hand or leaf by frond with ferns in most welcome patterns of beauty. Many ferns will be happy with just

27

those soil conditions and sites that are chosen to persuade hostas to perform at their best. Moisture rather than drought rules in places where some shade at least is allowed rather than the unrelenting baking of the sun. Broad, undivided patterns of leaves arranged in an informal bouquet, often crowded and close to the ground, make the hostas one of our leading foliage plants. Distinct from ferns, they have some of their classical feeling, but they have leaves of different texture and form that provide contrast but not in too glaring a manner. Even the variegation that many cultivars engage in is managed without too extrovert and carnival a spirit, a sartorial adventure of dignified distinction. Such refined use of colour is effective in the hostas alone, but is given extra point against the ferns which, with very rare exceptions, do not adopt any form of variegation.

WOODLAND

Ferns are possessed of a magical aura. But this is not something they hug to themselves; they quickly create an atmosphere all around and nowhere is this more telling than in light woodland. Here one enters a new world, it envelops one; above and all around the vegetation dominates, and the right ferns planted here can be really bewitching. They may grow to their optimum size and beauty, undisturbed by either over-enthusiastic gardeners hoeing the soil and destroying shallow roots or by less kindly aspects of the weather. Partial shade will be welcomed, but so too will the shelter from wind which can be one of the main hazards of some of the most intricate and splendid cultivars. Nor need one have acres of woodland to manage this woodland atmosphere. A group of three trees suitably planted around will create the magic, and where space is at a real premium a solitary tree with shrubs can be effective.

A very telling picture can be created by inter-

planting some of the evergreen polypody ferns, *Polypodium vulgare* forms, with the autumn-flowering hardy cyclamen, *C. hederifolium* and especially the vivid white form. The bright clean shining green of the ferns and the magic lantern flowers of the cyclamens is a refreshing and bright contrast of colour and form. A collection of snowdrops growing alongside both deciduous and evergreen ferns provides an equally appealing combination, the snowdrop foliage disappearing as the deciduous ferns unfurl their new fronds. Hart's tongue ferns and snowdrops complement each other delightfully. Later bluebells can be in bloom as the earlier deciduous ferns have freshly broken into growth and so together engage in a piece of ever-fresh garden theatre. Even the simple picture of evergreen ferns holding their bright green fronds proudly among the rusted fallen leaves of autumn is always an attractive picture, natural and uncontrived and all the better for being so.

DRY AREAS

There is a number of small species that are found growing on walls, sometimes where it is difficult to see how roots can penetrate apparently perfectly sound cement mortar. In stone walls with older and crumbling mortar, or where the absence of mortar is made good by a little soil and detritus, some of these little plants can form substantial colonies. Their homes must at times be exceedingly arid and the plants hard-pressed to survive despite long-ranging roots. The very pleasing rusty-back fern, *Asplenium ceterach* (*Ceterach officinarum*), is very drought resistant (Fig. 8). The fronds curl up into what looks like a dried wasted piece of material at times, but with a shower of rain they unfurl apparently undamaged and ready to carry on growing. Plants may spread happily but will rarely be more than 5–10 cm (2–4 in) high.

Other wall dwellers include the pretty little common

or maidenhair spleenwort, *Asplenium trichomanes*, the usual form of which will relish the lime it finds in old mortar, but there is a look-alike subspecies that is a lime-hater (Fig. 9). While it is fun to have these little plants growing on walls, they can also be grown in rock beds or sink gardens. The tiny dark wall spleen-wort, *Asplenium ruta-muraria*, is more difficult away from walls; it may well be best to resist any attempt to grow this anywhere else. Other spleenworts can be relied on to manage in very dry spots and can be useful in rock gardens or rock beds. The black spleen-wort, *Asplenium adiantum-nigrum*, is a popular neat plant usually under 30 cm (1 ft) high and with dark, neatly divided fronds which are polished and of very thick texture.

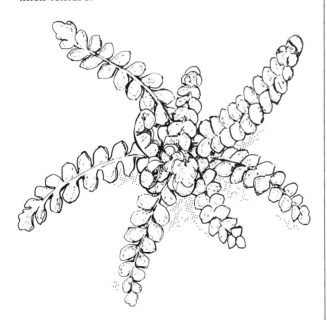

Fig. 8 *Asplenium ceterach*, the rusty-back fern.

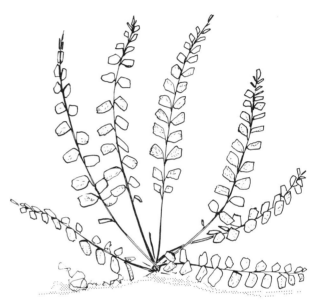

Fig. 9 *Asplenium trichomanes*, the maidenhair spleenwort.

SPECIMEN FERNS

Often ferns can make a dramatic point planted as single specimens alone on the stage or accompanied by very demure or low-growing planting such as creeping Jenny or, in drier situations, thymes and harebells. There will be no dispute about who is playing the star role. A waterside clump of the royal fern, *Osmunda regalis*, or the broad buckler fern, *Dryopteris dilatata*, will need no help to make a really fine solo effect.

29

The male fern, *Dryopteris filix-mas*, is a robust plant with many very good variants. These will all do well in semi-shaded situations and will manage very nicely in neutral or acid soils. Of many fine cultivars, *D.f-m.* 'Cristata Martindale' is a strong grower with each frond decorated with ornate crests at the ends of the fronds and at the end of each of the pinnae.

A relative to the last is the scaly male fern, *Dryopteris affinis* (*D. pseudomas*), described as 'scaly' because of the covering of coppery scales that decorate the new fronds in the spring. Of many variants one has been long known as the king fern. This is *D.a.* 'Cristata The King', a fertile kind of which the best forms are perhaps 1 m (3 ft) high with widely spreading fronds heavily crested at the end of each pinna and at the apex of each frond.

The soft shield fern, *Polystichum setiferum*, is a popular kind for planting in prominent positions as its light green, very intricately cut fronds are a delight as the orange crosiers unfurl or in full soft velvety maturity. In drier situations the plants will perhaps not reach over a pleasing 60 cm (2 ft) while being of basically horizontal design, but good forms grown in moist sheltered spots can be majestic at 1.5 m (5 ft). As it is likely to produce lots of small plantlets from the rachis, a single specimen can soon become a clump or a colony. But if a single clump is what one wants, it is no great hardship to remove the smaller offspring to other welcoming sites.

On a smaller scale one can make good use of a plant like the hart's tongue fern, *Asplenium scolopendrium*, in cool moist spots. It can be a very effective solitary specimen plant, quite quickly forming a large clump. It is a very accommodating plant, either as the type or one of its cultivars, as it can often be poked into corners where little else would flourish and provide punctuation along a path or at the base of a wall.

In light woodland very many ferns can be used in solitary splendour (Fig. 10). The shelter from wind will enable some of the more intricate lacy-fronded types such as some of the lady ferns (*Athyrium filix-femina* 'Victoriae' is a good example) to develop their full potential and make a splendid plant perhaps 1 m (3 ft) high and as much across.

COLONIZING FERNS

Mention has been made above of the colonizing propensity of the soft shield fern, *Polystichum setiferum*. If space allows a colony of these, perhaps five or more plants can look very distinctive. Grown in numbers the characteristics of the fern are emphasized. Perhaps the best known colonizer is the very popular shuttlecock or ostrich feather fern, *Matteuccia struthiopteris*. This is another plant that will adapt its size to its conditions, upright fronds reaching some 40–50 cm (16–20 in) in spartan areas, but with plenty of moisture can reach 1–1.5 m (3–5 ft). Wherever they are placed they are likely to send out plenty of creeping black rooting rhizomes. Along these at intervals they produce new clusters of fronds to start fresh independent plants. This robust species is at its best in moist acid soils, and at its most prolific in loamy conditions. Anyone with the space will allow it quite a bit of freedom but there may come a time, fairly soon, when the hoe is brought into play to ensure a sensible limit to its territorial ambitions. It is a species which has contentedly naturalized outside its native habitats and in places it has made itself at home with very impressive stands by pools and lakes.

Blechnum spicant is commonly called the ladder fern because of the regular rung-like disposition of the undivided pinnae. It is a native British plant that can be

North wall site with hart's tongue fern, *Asplenium scolopendrium*, happy in the company of ivies.

Fig. 10 Plant associations: birches, rhodo-dendrons, dogwood, hostas, pulmonarias with ferns.

found growing on shady moist rocky spots or on the floor of woods. In cultivation it soon makes a wide clump. It is, of course, very hardy, and so too is *Adiantum venustrum* from parts of the Himalayas and Canada. Its triangular to ovate fronds measure 15–30 cm (6–12 in) long and start bright apple green but become bluey green with maturity.

While a number of species such as the shuttlecock fern will quickly cover a wide area of ground if given half a chance, most are more circumspect, even among those that like to form colonies. *Adiantum pedatum* is such a one and perhaps would be among the first ten to be recommended to a beginner. It is certainly a distinct kind. Its creeping rhizomes steadily extend the size of the clump. Producing lots of rigidly upright purple black stems it arranges its fronds almost horizontally some 30 cm (12 in) or so from the ground. The stems are as thin as threads but very strong. The fronds have lots of evenly sized oblong pinnules like fan blades, arranged apparently on some subtle aerodynamic principle. The blade of each of these horizontal fronds is about 10 cm (4 in) long. Plants develop as dense ground cover in the humus and moisture they relish.

ADAPTABLE FERNS

The male fern, *Dryopteris filix-mas*, is probably one of the most widespread of fern species, being found throughout the whole of Europe including Britain, in Central and North America as well as in Asia. It is undemanding in its requirements, growing wild in our woodlands, lanes, hedgerows and open heathland. In any of these places it will manage on really very poor dry tack. This is one of the species that has given rise to many named cultivars which all have the same strong constitution and can exist nicely where other kinds might falter. While the type is a strong, large extrovert, many of the mutant cultivars are much smaller and can be incorporated into planting designs where the type would be much too much of a good thing.

Another very widely distributed fern is the common polypody, *Polypodium vulgare*, which does best in humus-rich soils that are very well drained. In the wild it can be found around the bases of trees like oaks, even climbing up moister boles by way of fissures in the bark. It can run over the stones or bricks of old walls and perhaps cover them completely if there has been a layer of detritus or moss laid down for the creeping rootstocks to make their way through. It is found quite frequently in hedgerows that have been unmolested by sprayers and tidy-minded gardeners. Some of the mutant kinds are very interesting and attractive; they are adaptable and have even been used in hanging baskets.

If one grows some of the lady ferns, *Athyrium filix-femina*, near the male ferns, the idea of gender difference becomes clear: the lady fern forms are somewhat lighter and more delicately graceful than the male ferns, and the light airy effect is exaggerated in some cultivars such as *A.f-f.* 'Victoriae', with long narrow fronds in some cases over 1 m (3 ft) long and with very narrow pinnae precisely paired to make crosses. Pinnae and fronds are ended with tasselled crests. It is a fertile kind so it makes sense to pick out a good example of 'Victoriae' and then perhaps to plant in a group or groups of three.

FERNS IN MIXED COMMUNITIES

There may be sites in the garden that seem so suited to fern culture that one quickly succumbs to the idea of planting up a collection of ferns – and indeed the next chapter is devoted to the creation of a fernery. But most gardeners, while perhaps admitting special favourites, are likely to be interested in a wide range of plants and will want to create a garden landscape

33

that looks well at all times of the year and is very varied. Ferns are ideal plants in mixed communities, they obviously usually grow in mixed vegetation in the wild. Expanses of unaccompanied bracken are the exception to the usual disposition of ferns to work with all sorts of plants and perhaps to benefit from the activities of these other characters. The shade afforded by some will help, the shelter from wind will aid others, the leafy detritus that turns to leaf mould will help most. Ferns in their turn can help their neighbours.

Part of the garden stage is swept bare for winter but becomes lively before spring arrives, and through the early months of the gardener's year is decorated by a succession of bulbous plants. Snowdrops and winter aconites are accompanied or rapidly followed by early crocuses, scillas, chionodoxas, muscari, small tulips and early daffodils. It is a bit of stage craft repeatedly performed in our gardens, but is always fresh and exciting. The foliage of these smaller bulbs is no great eyesore as it is dying down, but neither is it a matter of any very great beauty. If ferns occupy the same ground they will come into active growth just after the bulbs have finished and take a more commanding presence on the stage as the bulbs' foliage wastes away. Almost nothing could be more neatly arranged.

Ferny blades of many types can contrast well with the foliage, form and flowers of herbaceous and shrubby plants; they can also maintain a sense of decorum when some colourful floral exhibitionists are perhaps at war with their pigments. The ferns provide a buffer zone between the colours and of course have a timeless feeling of order and design that adds gravitas to the whole and will certainly be more lasting than the passing *joie de vivre* of plants with seasonal floral displays. The corner of a bed or border can be made dramatic by the planting of a strong-growing fern such as one of the interesting male ferns able to stand up like Horatio at the bridge and let no one pass without stopping to admire. You might try the very strong *Dryopteris filix-mas* 'Grandiceps Wills', standing some 60 cm (2 ft) or more tall with bold fronds decorated with crested pinnae and large terminal extravaganzas, hugely decorative flourishes in the form of crests. A single plant will soon be a bustling scrum of crowns.

Some good border plants are not outstanding foliage plants: alliums, while respectable in youth will often allow their foliage to become tired with burnt-off ends before the flowers have begun to open. The ferns cast an attractive veil over such wayward behaviour.

The bare ground below a specimen tree can be transformed by a colony of *Polypodium vulgare* 'Cambricum' or 'Cornubiense'. A moist spot can be given over to the hart's tongue fern, not a single specimen but some dozens, with groups of the very interesting mutant forms.

In semi-shade drifts of lady ferns will look wonderful for months and quite often throughout the year. They can be made to look even more exciting by sub-letting some of their ground space to groups of lilies. You could try *L. martagon* on any soils including limy ones. These same soils could support the wonderful yellow *L. szovitsianum* or the later flowering orange *L. henryi*. The stylized foliage of *L. pardalinum*, the leopard lily, produced in whorls at intervals up the stems will, with the nodding brilliant red and golden spotted flowers, make a notable contrast to the delicacy of the ferns. Many other lilies will enter into a marriage of convenience with ferns, benefiting from the cool shade round their roots that a colony of ferns will provide.

Popular soft shield fern, *Polystichum setiferum*, looking well contrasted to formal pathway and falling greenery of winter-flowering jasmine, *Jasminum nudiflorum*.

Where labour saving is an element in the gardening equation, ferns can hold their own with the best. A mixed planting of shrubs and ferns makes sense and magic. Rhododendrons look extremely well-matched with ferns growing among them, the somewhat heavy foliage being lightened by the ferns' lighter touch.

FERNS IN CONTAINERS

This book is not concerned with ferns grown under glass or inside, whether or not they are hardy, but outside ferns can be grown in pots and other containers. This gives us the advantage of mobility. The ferns may be brought into prominence when they are at their most interesting and attractive; deciduous ones can be moved off-stage through the winter. One method of using potted ferns where space is very limited is to sink the whole pot into the garden for the summer, perhaps following a sunken potful of tulips or daffodils that has passed out of blooming.

As ferns are not happy to have their roots disturbed or to dry out it follows that, within reason, the bigger the pot they are housed in the happier they are likely to be. They will need repotting at intervals, the more vigorous ones perhaps annually. To minimize the effect of root disturbance the best time to do the job is in spring or early summer when they are ready to grow vigorously. Pots can become a mass of roots quite quickly. Some indication of their activity can be gauged by the fact that some indoor ferns need repotting every six months.

Almost any of the hardy ferns will grow well in pots using suitable compost and provided they are shaded and not allowed to dry out. While a fern in full growth can be brought into a prominent position on the patio for special occasions, if this is a sunny or windswept spot, the pot should be moved back into a more sheltered spot after its outing. Drying and battering wind is one of the main dangers to many ferns.

Under glass many ferns can be grown in hanging baskets, and some of the hardy kinds can be used in the same way outside, provided again that they are not placed in a wind tunnel and are carefully managed. Certainly they make a change from lobelia, petunias and fuchsias, although it is perfectly possible to have such colourful plants, especially trailing kinds, alongside the ferns.

CHAPTER 4

Creating a Fernery

Ferneries are not quite the current 'in' thing, but they could be one of the garden fashions of the nineties. There is no doubt about the increasing interest in the plants; books and articles abound and more and more nurserymen and garden centres are beginning to list at least a few of the numerous kinds. Whether this renaissance will lead to the creation of ferneries is perhaps a debatable point; I feel that it is likely for several reasons.

These reasons can be simply listed. Ferns are beautiful. There is a wide choice of kinds that are easy to grow. They will virtually manage themselves and can be grown in many sites that are not all that attractive to many other plants. Damp and shaded or semi-shaded areas that are very suitable for ferns are likely to be more plentiful as houses and other buildings take up a greater proportion of living space. The plants do not necessarily need very deep soils; they are basically surface-rooting, relying on a considerable number of roots working on an egalitarian basis – they have no equivalent of the tap root or the main roots of most flowering plants.

Should a portion of ground be designated 'the fernery' and devoted more or less exclusively to these plants, what might the drawbacks be? It would be less than honest to suggest that all ferns are equally interesting and attractive every month of the year. The majority of hardy kinds are deciduous, some more so than others. There are evergreen ones, but even these are probably at their most lively when the new fronds are unfurling or have just spread themselves out through the spring and early summer. So the impact of a fernery is lessened in winter. But I am not convinced that the lesser winter appeal is a huge handicap. Less time is spent out in the garden during the winter and much can be done to make the fernery pleasing in these months without resorting to planting it with a plethora of plastic gnomes!

The concept

The idea is a simple one. A fernery is an area devoted to the culture of ferns. There may or may not be other plants present, but any strangers will play a very secondary role. In gardening terms it is often a convenience as well as a visually effective plan to mass forces, to bring together collections of plants of a genera or family within sections of the garden. The rose garden is the most popular example, but irises, peonies, heathers and many other plants can be similarly honoured. There is, however, a difference of quality. Ferns have an age-long history and have their own rules of growth, propagation and leaf structure. They are set apart from the rest of vegetative creation in rather a similar way to that of the fauna and flora of Australasia, which might belong to another planet so different is it from the rest of the world's living things. There is enormous appeal in creating a small garden populated solely by these curiosities of the plant world.

Making a hardy fernery

There may be many attitudes towards this venture. Size will depend on inclination and available suitable space. A very pleasing collection can be housed on normal flat ground but a sloping area allows greater scope for the display of the plants and the matching of sites to species. There is much to be said in favour of the traditional plan for a fernery and this is now detailed.

SITE

The ideal site will be moist and cool. It will be protected from strong sunlight and from the damaging effects of blustery winds. An area shaded by buildings or tall deciduous trees may meet the shade and shelter requirements. The lie of the land will vary but one which does not receive direct sunlight will prove excellent, being also an aspect not favoured by most other types of plants.

In the siting and layout of the fernery top priority should be to provide a series of microclimates that will suit a whole series of different ferns. What none of them wants is searing winds; the ravine should be a place of calm not a wind-funnel. Shelter from buildings, from trees and from clumps of shrubs will all help, and any winding 'valleys' built into the form of the structure will be beneficial. The careful siting of clumps of larger and more robust ferns where they will help temper the wind to the shorn lambs, and provide a peaceful haven for more delicate cultivars.

FORMATION

The design of the fernery is going to involve to a greater or lesser degree the reshaping of the plot as it has been inherited from Nature, the last owners or the builders. The form of the ground and rock cover will then be further exploited by the sensitive planting of the ferns themselves and possibly some associated non-fern plants.

One of the bolder ferns, like this male fern, can be used as strong punctuation in a border, perhaps as here on the corner where it also helps to soften a hard border outline.

Fig. 11 Fernery construction. Effort is made to create shaded and moist planting sites.

If it is possible to create the effect of a mini-ravine this will have many benefits. The drainage is likely to be easily managed, but with very much moister conditions towards the bottom, so that species with differing moisture requirements can be sensibly stationed. The steep slopes will also make it very much easier to examine and enjoy the ferns once they are established, as many will be closer to eye level – a consideration that all will appreciate and certainly those of more mature years (Fig. 11).

The ravine effect can be achieved by exaggerating any natural changes of soil level by manual effort or by hiring a calfdozer to push and manipulate the soil until you have the contours that please. Rocks can be an integral part of the design and if laid out well will give pleasure even in the winter when there will be less to be contributed by the collection of ferns. The basic rules of rock garden construction should be observed so that there is not the constant irritation of some ridiculous contradiction in the strata of rocks laid. The stumps of felled trees are often utilized to provide shelter and suitable microclimates for some ferns. They are likely to become covered with a selection of mosses that will look well – and could provide a further field for study!

Even a small valley, ravine or bankside will look more natural if the lines are curving rather than straight, so that the eye is led forward to the partially or completely hidden section beyond. Where space allows the pathway may divide so that there are two valleys.

PATHS

Along the bottom of our ravines will be the pathway along which we and our admiring visitors will travel. The lower ground will attract maximum moisture and is where rain will collect, so that the path needs to take account of this and allow for very good drainage. If the path is made of stone or paving stones it should be borne in mind that the conditions are likely to encourage the growth of algae and mosses and so create a surface that, when moist, can be treacherous underfoot. We do not want to create a hazard to life and limb. If stones are securely mounted on a good depth of clean gravel and their edges are proud of the surrounding gravel or soil one should be safe. Alternatively the path may be made of some suitable gravel laid over a clean-draining hardcore base.

Planting

While any landmoving operations may take place any time that suits, the planting up of the fernery is likely to be more successful in getting the plants established more quickly if undertaken either in early autumn or spring. In a mild winter it may well be possible to continue planting some of the stronger kinds quite late in the season. Where there is any doubt, and certainly where the fernery is in a rather open, exposed site or in a cold area, it may be wiser to choose spring as the main planting time, when most ferns will be becoming much more active in their roots prior to unfurling new fronds.

The majority of ferns will manage in a fairly wide variety of soils, not hugely objecting to a range of soil structures or a fairly wide band of pH levels, but most probably do best in slightly acid soils of an open loam enlivened with leaf mould. Further advice on preparing the soil is given in Chapter 5.

DISPOSITION OF FERNS

First an elementary word of warning. Ferns sold by specialists, garden centres and other outlets will usually be young plants looking very sweet and small in modestly sized pots. Because these young plants

41

look just like miniature adults, they may give a false impression of the dimensions of the plant in maturity. One can even find the royal fern, *Osmunda regalis*, looking demure in a 8cm (3in) pot, giving no indication of the possible 1–2m (3–6ft) height and greater spread that it can soon achieve. Responsible dealers will have some indication of mature sizes on labels or display cards, but we have all heard of baby alligators being sold as pets, or tiny puppies that have grown to difficult dimensions. It can happen with ferns if we are not careful.

While there are a lot of small ferns that can be planted quite close together, many of the medium and larger ones are going to need plenty of room; they will look far better with some air space around each specimen rather than crowded like travellers in the rush hour.

We have the terrain in front of us, we have a selection of ferns to be planted. We act as generals disposing our forces to the best effect, taking account of soil conditions, of aspect, of the ultimate sizes of the specimens and of their colours, forms and characters.

Perhaps first of the considerations when sorting out the plants is to achieve a balance of deciduous and evergreen kinds so that no area becomes devoid of growing interest for the winter months – or at least to ensure that the most obvious and most important sites are well-furnished with interest throughout the year (Figs. 12 & 13).

There can be quite dramatic differences of texture and of colour. The hard polished surfaces of the hart's tongue are totally distinct from the soft velvety feel

Pond surrounded with moisture-loving plants, ferns, blue *Iris sibirica* and yellow *Iris pseudacorus*, trollius and astilbes. The silver-leaved tree is the useful willow-leaved pear, *Pyrus salicifolia*.

and look of some of the cultivars of the soft shield fern, *Polystichum setiferum*.

In colour there are interesting changes through the life of many species. New young foliage may be very much brighter and lighter than adult foliage. One of the most attractively coloured is *Dryopteris erythrosorus*, with young fronds a shining copper-tinted pink or pale orange. As it continues to produce fresh fronds for a considerable part of the year there are usually the younger flushed fronds contrasting to the more sober older ones. The new fronds of *Dryopteris wallichiana* are almost golden, a colour made even more eye-catching by the dark, near-black rachis. In contrast, *Adiantum venustrum* can look blue-rinsed in maturity. *Athyrium nipponicum pictum* has burgundy coloured rachis and pinnae midribs, while the pinnae are grey merging to green at the edges, and even the standard male fern is really a light green in some forms but notably darker in others, like *Dryopteris filix-mas* 'Depauperata' with narrow pinnae and fronds a dark polished colour.

To contrast the colours will be almost as important as displaying the varying growth habits of associated kinds. Size and solidity of one kind can be emphasized by the petite growth and delicacy of neighbours. Some, like many *Polystichum setiferum* forms, have spreading, intricate fronds at low angles close to the horizontal, while the ostrich feather fern, *Matteuccia struthiopteris*, is upright, imitating its other common name of shuttlecock fern. Many start displaying the blades of their fronds close to the base of the rootstock; others, like *Adiantum pedatum*, have their fronds held aloft by erect stems and the larger-scale *Dryopteris dilatata* will start its wide triangular fronds well clear of its rootstock.

Allow for the colonizing abilities of some, and the increasing clump size of others. Larger kinds will contrast with ground-cover, creeping kinds like the

Fig. 12 Wet and waterside plant associations. Hostas, ligularias, reeds, grasses, calthas, irises with ferns: 1. *Dryopteris dilatata* **2.** *D. filix-mas* **3.** *Asplenium scolopendrium* **4.** *Polystichum setiferum* **5.** *Osmunda regalis.*

Fig. 13 Plant associations: conifers, rhododendrons, Virginia creeper, hostas, bergenias etc. 1. *Matteuccia struthiopteris* **2.** *Dryopteris filix-mas* **'Cristata' 3.** *Polystichum setiferum* **4.** *Dryopteris dilatata* **5.** *Athyrium filix-femina.*

attractive *Blechnum penna-marina*, which in friable moist shady spots will spread very swiftly and make a dense pattern of neat narrow fronds. Although this enjoys a moist spot it is one of the kinds that can stand up to a large ration of sunshine.

The overall unity of feeling of ferns means that it is difficult to make real blunders in contrasting their characters, but, while the overall principle of design is governed by the need to make the most of each specimen by contrasting it with dissimilar kinds, one does not want to end with a spotty effect even in a modestly sized planting. Much can be done to avoid this by planting some of the small or medium ones in groups of three or five. This helps to give a more cohesive feel to the whole and certainly does not preclude us from having single specimens both large and small. One or two strong ferns may be placed in rather more prominent exposed positions, sentinels guarding the whole area.

A smallish fernery may not allow the indulgence of planting a shrub or two or perhaps introducing a few of the smaller lilies. One can make much of the inviolated purity of the planting, but where space permits I am not so sure that an odd shrub and stray clump of flowering plants does not somehow emphasize the fern-ness of the ferns!

SELECTING THE FERNS

The choice is very wide, but in the end the final selection is going to depend on such practical factors as available space and soil conditions together with personal preferences. Each enthusiast may have a different set of plants in his or her collection but if

In a shaded border a number of ferns can look well much of the year and be interplanted with bulbs such as snowdrops, small daffodils and early herbaceous flowers such as hellebores.

47

called on for a restricted list it is likely that there will be a common core. Chapter 7 describes briefly many of the available hardy ferns, but here are some kinds, grouped by height, that could be useful in various ways. But first a list that could make a good starter collection.

Top ten

Adiantum pedatum American maidenhair
Asplenium scolopendrium hart's tongue
Athyrium filix-femina 'Victoriae' lady fern form
Dryopteris affinis 'Cristata The King' scaly male fern form
Dryopteris erythrosorus autumn fern
Dryopteris filix-mas 'Cristata Martindale' male fern form
Matteuccia struthiopteris ostrich feather fern
Osmunda regalis royal fern (*or*, less huge but still impressive, any good form of *Dryopteris dilatata*)
Polystichum setiferum 'Divisilobum Iveryanum' soft shield fern form
Polystichum setiferum 'Pulcherrimum Bevis' soft shield fern form

Dwarf ferns: 8–30 cm (3–12 in) high

Asplenium adiantum-nigrum black spleenwort
Asplenium ceterach rusty-back fern
Asplenium ruta-muraria wall rue
Asplenium scolopendrium 'Marginata Irregulare' hart's tongue form
Asplenium trichomanes maidenhair spleenwort
Asplenium viride green-ribbed spleenwort
Athyrium filix-femina 'Congestum Minus' (and other dwarf forms of lady fern)

Blechnum penna-marina alpine water fern
Gymocarpium dryopteris plumosum oak fern form
Polypodium vulgare 'Cornubiense' common polypody form
Polystichum setiferum 'Congestum' (and other dwarf forms of soft shield fern)
Polystichum tsus-simense
Woodsia obtusa
Woodwardia radicans 'Angustifolia'

Medium ferns: 30–60 cm (12–24 in) high

Adiantum pedatum American maidenhair
Asplenium scolopendrium forms hart's tongue
Athyrium filix-femina in many forms lady fern
Dryopteris erythrosorus autumn fern
Dryopteris filix-mas in many forms male fern
Dryopteris marginalis marginal shield fern
Onoclea sensibilis sensitive fern
Polypodium vulgare and forms common polypody
Polystichum acrostichoides Christmas fern
Polystichum aculeatum forms prickly shield fern
Polystichum setiferum in many forms soft shield fern
Woodwardia radicans

Larger ferns: over 60 cm (24 in)

Athyrium felix-femina in many forms lady fern
Blechnum chilense
Dryopteris filix-mas in many forms male fern
Dryopteris goldiana
Dryopteris wallichiana
Matteuccia struthiopteris ostrich fern
Osmunda regalis royal fern
Osmunda spectabilis
Polystichum aculeatum prickly shield fern

CHAPTER 5

Growing Hardy Ferns

What ferns like

Some mention has been made of the conditions ferns enjoy. Requirements vary but there are several common factors.

Above all others, there is one thing that ferns need. This is a stable root environment. They are shallow-rooting plants and resent their roots being disturbed, so extensive hoeing around them is bad policy. Whilst some strong species can be lifted and pulled apart into several pieces as a sensible method of propagation, to many kinds overcoming this cavalier treatment will take a long time to accomplish, and to some this rough division will be instant death.

Whilst there are kinds that grow in the most exposed places, on the whole ferns enjoy a degree of protection from high winds. Certainly the larger kinds with delicate fronds can be spoilt by being continually buffeted by wind. Some ferns protect themselves a little from excessive transpiration by curling up their fronds, but this does give them a pinched look – rather like holiday-makers shrouded with rainwear in poor weather.

To look their best they also need space. Young ferns can look charming even as small plants as sold by nurserymen, but make sure that you leave enough for the established mature plant to spread its fronds without hindrance. A crowded fern can look miserable in the same way that a cat caught in a rainstorm looks a travesty of its normal elegant self. They are certainly companionable plants that look better for the contrast of differing neighbours, but do not crowd them.

Dislikes may be similarly listed and cultivars will have graduated responses to these.

Enemy number one is strong sunlight. Even an hour or so of hot sunshine can hurt more delicate kinds by scorching fronds and creating bleached patches or causing new growth to shrivel. Such damage can be aggravated by attendant factors like drying winds, lack of humidity and lack of soil moisture.

Wind can be a major problem, blowing the fronds back and forth and causing them to be bruised or broken. Even a steady breeze can reduce the humidity and dry out the fronds, especially the vulnerable younger ones. The wind-tunnel effect that can occur between buildings can rule out what might be otherwise a good site.

Some ferns are well adapted to survive dry spells but dryness at the roots is death to many and to others will cause discomfort, seen in the unhappy, shrunken appearance of the fronds.

Very cold weather coming as an unexpected spell during growing periods will stop growth and adversely affect some less robust kinds. Frost will stop active growth at the end of the season, but a severe one after growth has got under way in the spring can turn new fronds black and require the plants to make a fresh start. Mild frosts at this time may well be survived without damage if the plants have some shelter from the neighbouring buildings or shrubs and trees. Some species that can achieve evergreen status in mild winters will quickly become deciduous if harder conditions arrive.

As a general rule, then, ferns like shade, humidity, shelter from wind, constant fresh, non-stagnant soil moisture, open soil structure with adequate oxygen, free soil drainage and a high humus content in the top-soil. Each species or cultivar may be more or less tolerant of different levels of these factors, especially sunlight, moisture and wind. In the individual descriptions in Chapter 7 note is made of these requirements.

Preparing the soil

Although one or two ferns, such as the pretty parsley fern, *Cryptogramma crispa*, inhabit screes, this is an unusual habitat for a fern, as it is so poorly provided with the humus that most demand. As ferns like to have a well-aerated soil it follows that very heavy clays are also bad news. The structure of heavy clays will be improved by the particle-flocking action stimulated by dressings of lime. Organic matter will help to make all soils more lively and the beneficial effects of earthworms make their significant contribution. Heavy clays often suffer from having thin topsoil so that all that can be done to build this up to combat clay's compacting inclination will be to the good. Deep digging will improve structure and drainage especially if straw, bracken waste minus the roots, and almost any form of organic material is dug in. Builders' rubble put well down is not harmful.

Pure sands are as unfriendly – they tend to dry out quickly and have little or no humus. Like heavy soils, light sands can be much improved by cultivation, especially by incorporating lots of humus as well-rotted compost, grass cuttings, leaf mould or shredded organic matter. Open soil is going to dry out on the surface quickly, so a mulch of leaves, shredded bark or other humus-rich detritus will keep the surface-rooting ferns cool and moist.

A community of ferns including hart's tongue, *Asplenium scolopendrium*, and *Adiantum pedatum* growing in shade with lily of the valley below a beech tree.

While ferns enjoy moisture, they mostly hate stagnant water. If your proposed site is likely to hold water for long periods it would be advisable to lay drainage pipes down to take away the excess to some lower point or into a drainage system. In the previous chapter it was suggested that a ravine-type contour would be suitable for a fernery; this may entail excavating soil and this could be used to build up levels around and so improve drainage. Paths at the bottom of such 'ravines' can be laid on a generous depth of drainage material and further improve the ferny environment.

As the soil down below is not going to be explored much by the fern roots, its management should be such as to support a healthy top spit. The top 15–25 cm (6–10 in) of soil can be concentrated upon and a generous allowance of compost made up of approximately 2 parts good loam or rottted turf, 1 part leaf mould and 1 part grit or coarse sand (clean of clay particles) would be beneficial. Repeated mulching of the surface will quickly encourage the soil bacteria and earthworms to increase their numbers and activity. The mulches will have the effect of giving the topsoil a better structure, one that will retain moisture better and usually add to the acidity content.

As a generalization ferns grow well on neutral or slightly acid soils. While at first this may seem to preclude their culture in chalky areas it is not necessarily so. There are many acid-loving plants to be found growing in chalklands, where the important topsoil has been turned acid and its acidity maintained by the continued dropping of tree leaves. The gardener can follow this lead. There are also some ferns that are positive lime lovers. Some of the more notable ones are listed. (Not all of these species are readily available, but should be obtainable from specialist nurseries. Details of the more common species are given in Chapter 7.)

Lime lovers

Adiantum reniforme
Asplenium adiantum-nigrum
Asplenium ceterach
Asplenium fontanum
Asplenium resiliens
Asplenium rhizophyllum
Asplenium ruta-muraria
Asplenium scolopendrium
Asplenium trichomanes
Asplenium viride
Cryptogramma crispa
Cyrtomium falcatum
Cystopteris bulbifera
Cystopteris fragilis
Dryopteris ludoviciana
Gymnocarpium robertianum
Matteuccia struthiopteris
Pellaea atropurpurea
Polypodium australe
Polypodium vulgare
Polystichum aculeatum

Planting and choosing plants

Probably the best times for planting will be early autumn, allowing plenty of time for the plants to get rooted into the surrounding soil before winter, or in the spring just when the roots are becoming active. My own preference is to plant in the early spring.

Ferns are grown for sale in pots and available year round, so many of the stronger ones can be added during the growing months, from spring until the first autumn frosts.

The choice will be between young plants in 8 cm (3 in) pots and very much larger and more expensive specimens in 15- or even 20-cm (6–8 in) pots. Unless

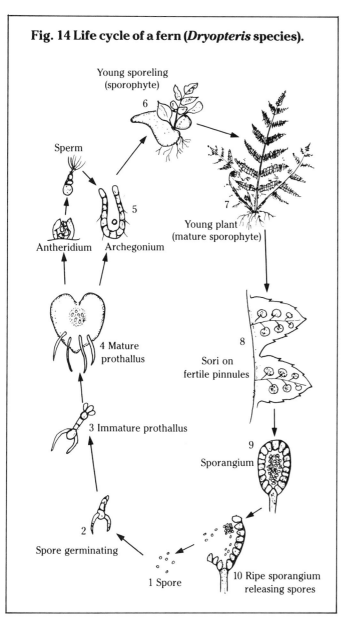

Fig. 14 Life cycle of a fern (*Dryopteris* species).

Young sporeling
(sporophyte)
6

7 Young plant
(mature sporophyte)

Sperm

5

Antheridium   Archegonium

4 Mature
prothallus

Sori on
fertile pinnules
8

3 Immature prothallus

9
Sporangium

2

Spore germinating

1 Spore

10 Ripe sporangium
releasing spores

you have good reason to want a mature look immediately, there is little really to be gained by choosing larger plants. Try to pick out specimens that look fresh, that are growing strongly without being hopelessly potbound, and which have the character that you want.

This last point is more important with some named cultivars than others. Most ferns on offer will be clones or very uniform specimens raised from spores. Some spore-fertile kinds do vary a little, however, so it is worth trying to pick out the best-looking plants, perhaps those that show the neatest or most intricate leaf divisions. This may not always be very easy as young plants do not always reflect exactly the appearance that will be adopted by the mature plant. However, it is rather like ducks – it is difficult to find an ugly or unpleasing one!

While still not around in huge numbers, there is an increasing number of nurseries specializing in ferns now, and even your local garden centre may be beginning to stock some of the more common varieties of ferns. Specialist firms will be expert on the raising of ferns and usually give all the information that buyers need, but garden centres may not be so careful and their staff less knowledgeable.

The main point is to make sure that the ferns chosen are hardy; many attractive ferns sold in small pots are only suitable for frost-proof indoor culture. On the other hand, garden centre selections will sometimes concentrate on the male fern, *Dryopteris filix-mas* and the lady fern, *Athyrium filix-femina*; both are attractive but, being strong-growing, wild types, they may be bolder than you want. Although they will be splendid in spacious wild or larger woodland gardens, they will grow too vigorously in smaller gardens, taking up room that could be more interestingly planted with less robust forms of these and other species.

Propagation

Ferns may be propagated in several ways, including by spores, plantlets, bulbils, offsets, layering or simple division.

BY SPORES

In nature the usual method of increase is by spores, very light dust-like particles that may be dispersed in huge numbers over very wide areas. While spores are like seeds in giving rise to totally separate, distinct new individuals, they are fundamentally dissimilar as they contain only half the number of chromosomes of the parent. When they find a suitable habitat and start into growth they give rise to green film-like prothallus, a complete plant generation from which sexual parts should arise. If fertilization takes place a small plant will arise and begin to produce roots, the prothallus having shrivelled away (Fig. 14).

Spores are produced from sori to be found on the underside of fertile fronds. In some species the fertile fronds look totally different from the normal fronds. The sori are usually small raised areas, sometimes rounded but each species tends to have a distinct shape. The colour may be a rusty orange but can be brown or black. When the spores are ripe they will be released in large numbers. A small sample piece of frond can be taken from the mother plant and laid on a clean piece of paper. If left to dry a while and then tapped the frond's sori should, if the spores are ripe, release the dust-like particles very freely. Spores can be stored in clean labelled envelopes or paper packets before being sown. Spores from various species become ripe at different times. Many spores remain

Polystichum setiferum **with companions on north-facing wall. Included in picture is the virginia creeper and winter-flowering *Viburnum tinus*.**

55

viable for months, a few have shorter lives, but best results are obtained from sowing fresh spores.

It is important to regard the raising of ferns from spores as a clinical procedure. There are always moss spores and other microscopic organisms present in the air, in sowing media and on pots. These have to be thwarted or they will smother the surfaces of the potted spores. The procedure is as follows:

1 Select a sowing medium, whichever is felt the most convenient. Commercial growers are likely to use a mix of 1 part peat and 2 parts coarse sand or grit. This should be sterilized.

2 Wash out pots, new ones being preferable. Use earthenware pots if they are to be placed in the oven (see 4 below).

3 Use grit or clean coarse sand for the bottom third or half of the pot. Then add sowing medium to within 1 cm ($\frac{1}{2}$ in) of top of pot. Shake level but do not press too hard.

4 Pour boiling water through a sieve over the potful until all is soaked and the sowing medium has become very hot. Alternatively the pot can be given 10 minutes in the microwave or placed for half an hour in a cool oven at 93°C (200°F).

5 Allow the pot to cool a little.

6 Lightly distribute spores over surface of growing medium. It is easier to pour them on to a sheet of paper and tap this gently, rather than sprinkling with the fingers, but they are very light, so avoid draughts and do not sneeze!

7 Spray with mist of previously boiled or distilled water.

8 Immediately seal top of pot with plastic cling-film.

9 Stand pot in container of clean water and cover with shading.

10 Keep warm. Most spores germinate most freely in the temperature bands of 24–28°C (75–85°F).

11 Spores may germinate after two or three weeks but may take longer. Keep the pots standing in some water and covered until you can see the first true small fronds appearing above the prothallus.

12 At this stage take away the plastic covering, maintain humidity, but allow small plants to become more hardened.

13 The usual mass of little plants can be pricked out in groups into trays or 8 cm (3 in) pots and grown on in a standard potting compost. They can be further divided as they grow. A plant that has nicely filled a 8 cm (3 in) pot will be ready to place into its garden site.

BY DIVISION

This may seem the most obvious way to propagate ferns. With many, such as the stronger *Dryopteris* and *Athyrium* forms, this can be done relatively easily in early spring. Divided portions with good amounts of roots can be planted directly into their positions and watered in. More delicate kinds may be planted in pots where they can be more carefully tended, keeping them in a cool, moist, humid area.

All old fronds, worn or damaged rhizomes and old or fractured roots should be removed when division takes place.

Often it is easier to divide a relatively young specimen than a very long established one. It can be a mistake to be too greedy in dividing, especially one of the rarer, more important kinds. One can congratulate oneself on the number of divisions only to find that they do not survive and one may have killed an old friend. Better to take just an odd piece or so from such a specimen.

Kinds like the ostrich feather fern, *Matteuccia struthiopteris*, with many running rhizomes giving rise to new plants will be easy to propagate, but one should only remove parts of such rootstocks that have well-rooted fresh young plants. Pieces of creeping rhizome without rooted plantlets may not give rise to fresh plants.

BY OTHER METHODS

Some ferns are so obliging as to produce a series of tiny plantlets on some of their fronds and others offer bulbils. The very attractive soft shield fern, *Polystichum setiferum*, is one which, when it has established itself, will often be prolific with embryo plants all along the frond midribs, the rachis, one at the base of each pinna. As the frond ages the bulbils grow with their own small fronds developing. In nature a proportion of these would become fresh plants as the parent frond begins to rot and be covered with humus detritus. On strong plants such as these species the process can be quickened by cutting away the whole frond when the plantlets look quite advanced and placing the frond in a tray of potting mixture. Keep relatively cool and moist until the little plants have rooted and are growing away.

Alternatively the fronds of a growing plant can be layered. Extra humus-rich soil can be worked in below a frond which is then securely pegged down. The young bulbils along the rachis soon form independent little plants.

The hart's tongue fern, *Asplenium scolopendrium*, offers an unusual method of increase (Fig. 15). It can be propagated by removing the old frond stems with swollen bases. While it is possible to use this method at any time from early spring through almost to the end of the summer, I have had most success from propagation in the spring. Even without any green blade, these swollen bases to the rachis will produce a series of little white bulbils if inserted in a mix of peat and coarse sand and kept moist and warm in a shaded position for some 5–12 weeks. The little bulbils will begin to develop roots and become independent plants. This is a particularly welcome trait for some of

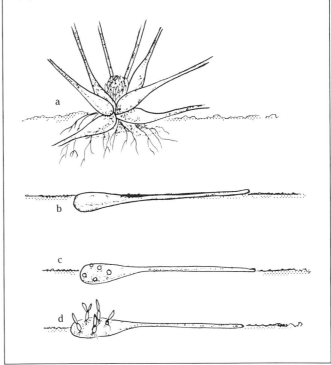

Fig. 15 Propagation of *Asplenium scolopendrium*. (a) Remove old stems (stripes) with swollen bases, the fronds having withered. (b) Stripe laid in moist mix of sand and peat or similar material. (c) White bulbils develop after 6–12 weeks. (d) Young plantlets developing.

the better forms of mutant kinds such as *A.s.* 'Crispum'.

Tissue culture is a possibility for those with a scientific bent but requires more equipment and resources than the average gardener possesses. Tubers are also a recognized form of increase for certain species, but not for any of the ferns normally grown for the ornamental garden.

CHAPTER 6

Round-the-Year Maintenance

The idea is simply to make the most of your ferns, to plant them in suitable positions where they will display themselves to their best advantage, and as part of the overall garden design to allow them to play their part by contributing their own beauty. We shall want to keep them growing healthily, affording us the means to increase them if we wish and to accentuate their best features, especially as they develop new fronds in the spring and early summer.

Most of the hardy ferns are remarkably easy to grow and many will survive years and even decades of neglect still looking well. Most of the routine culture matters are almost too obvious to mention, but even obvious things can get overlooked.

Watering

A steady supply of soil moisture and a humid atmosphere is what most ferns want. Hosing down with a strong jet from a hosepipe is likely to compact the soil and splash mud over the fronds. Very much better, if the soil and plants are in danger of becoming parched, is to rely on a sufficiently long dose of a light spray to moisten thoroughly the top few inches of soil. Certain areas may be kept rather more moist by laying down trickle irrigation, a pipe with regulated nozzles that allow a constant slow dribble of water. The supply can be turned on when needed. Young, newly planted specimens and propagated pieces will need to be looked after especially carefully to prevent their roots from drying out.

Establishing a topsoil that is protected from drying out with mulches of leaf mould, shredded bark, leaves and even gravel will be the most natural and prudent way not only to keep the roots moist and cool but to insulate from possibly traumatic fluctuations of temperatures.

Feeding

Most garden soils will contain all the nutrients that ferns need to grow, but to get them to really flourish it may be politic to feed them. Slow-release fertilizers are ideal, incorporated into the soil when planting and thereafter the natural feed from the soil and mulches can be augmented in the spring and early summer, just as ferns come into their really active period of fresh growth. No fertilizer should touch the ferns themselves.

Organic fertilizers will release their nutrients slowly over a long period; complete fertilizers like National Growmore are balanced mixes of inorganic chemicals that will be useful in complementing natural food. Such fertilizers will be particularly useful when and wherever dressings of shredded bark are applied, as uncomposted bark tends to entice the soil bacteria to work on the breaking down of their tissue, thereby leaving the soil rather thinly manned with bacteria and consequently with lower supplies of nitrogen being released.

Osmunda regalis, **the royal fern, in spring with crosiers unfurling; these can be 45–75 cm (18–30 in) long. Mature fronds may measure from 60 cm–1 m (2–3 ft) to a breathtaking 3–3.3 m (10–12 ft).**

Mulching

Mulches of all sorts of organic material are just what the ferns need. Most mulches will provide balanced feeding as the material turns to humus and is incorporated into the soil. Mulches can be applied from spring onwards. Incidentally a very good one can be made out of young, shredded bracken. It is particularly rich in potassium. The old browned fronds of bracken gathered at the end of the year may give a useful physical cover but will be less nutritious. Care should be taken not to introduce rooted pieces – best to enjoy bracken in the countryside, not in the garden.

The blanket effect of mulches means that they not only feed, but will keep soils moist and cool. As they get incorporated into the topsoil they will do a lot to change the texture of the soil and keep it healthily aerated. It is difficult to exaggerate the benefits of generous mulching with materials like well-rotted compost and leaf mould. They should also help to inhibit weed growth.

Weeding

Ferns do not like being messed about, especially around their roots. Hoeing weeds out will inevitably cut through large numbers of fern roots and considerably dent their performance. It makes sense to try to maintain a weed-free regime. Heavy mulches will make it child's play to pull out any weed that tries to associate itself with the ferns.

Obviously, any site infested with permanent or persistent weeds should be thoroughly cleaned prior to any planting. Should some really naughty weeds establish themselves among ferns and prove difficult to remove without causing severe disturbance the answer may well be to use a systemic weedkiller and to paint the weed leaves. However carefully used, a sprayer with a systemic weedkiller is likely to damage or kill the ferns as well as weeds.

Pruning

It may sound curious to talk of pruning ferns. What is suggested is that when the new fronds are just about to be unfurled it may be sensible to remove some of the older ones that are wasting away and rotting. This is often more easily and neatly done with a sharp pair of secateurs than pulling by hand. The old frond material can be composted. During the winter the fronds may look decorative, whether evergreen or as rusted deciduous parts, and they can do some good protecting the plant, but new growths are likely to look more impressive clear of any half-dead or completely dead material. It is not a matter of being excessively tidy, merely making the most of the drama of the new growths – and you may well think that some of the bolder kinds do not need this tidying operation. However if you start pulling and pruning when the young fronds are just uncurling you are likely to break some as they are very brittle – proceed with caution!

Thinning

Colonizing ferns such as the ostrich feather fern, *Matteuccia struthiopteris*, and the soft shield fern, *Polystichum setiferum*, can have population explosions and by becoming too crowded the full beauty of each plant can be spoilt. It makes sense to remove a number of the new plants and either start a fresh colony elsewhere, give them away to friends or help the funds of a local garden society or fund-raising event by putting them on their sales table.

Moving

Should ferns need moving, either because a specimen has grown too large for its position or because too many have grown together, whole established plants or youngsters can be moved successfully with a little care. Both large and small plants should be watered thoroughly before being dug up. They should be moved with the least possible root disturbance. Large plants will have a mass of roots, all close to the surface but extending quite widely. Plants can be lifted by being first dug widely around and being undermined with a spade. Each plant, freed of its connection with the soil, can be lifted or slid on to a sheet of strong polythene or something similar and pulled or wheeled away to the new site. It should be replanted immediately, to the same depth as before, maybe a couple of centimetres or an inch or so deeper to allow for soil settlement. Once in their new positions, plants and the surrounding soil should be watered and the surface mulched.

Maladies

When a fern looks unwell, check that the trouble is not simply that it is growing in an unsuitable position. Wind, strong sunlight, or too dry or alkaline a soil may be causing troubles. Root rot can be instigated by badly waterlogged soil. If such factors appear not to be at fault then it may be a matter of looking to the pests and diseases. Happily these are not too numerous for ferns – especially the outdoor hardy ones.

PESTS

Slugs and snails may enjoy the same moist conditions as ferns, but they are unlikely to be much of a nuisance as they will probably prefer lettuces and other goodies. The same tends to apply to caterpillars and even aphids. Traditional methods of controlling all these pests should suffice. Pyrethrum and Derris dusts, used as contact sprays, will control caterpillars and aphids if an infestation occurs. Certainly aphids can sometimes be a nuisance. They will cause some distortion and even prevent new fronds from unfurling if large numbers busy themselves sucking juices from the tenderest parts. A jet of water can help wash them away but surer destruction of the pest is effected by spraying with pyrethrum or similar insecticide.

DISEASES

These are not numerous, nor are they normally very serious in temperate parts of the world and among hardy ferns. The fungi which can attack all parts of a fern are a problem only in very warm, humid climates, and bacterial diseases are very rare.

Viruses may be suspected if there is distortion of leaf blades or stems and if fronds become patchily marked with paler colours in mosaic patterns. If a virus is suspected it would be wise to consult an expert. There is no cure for virus diseases; infected plants should be burnt.

Seasonal diary

Late winter
Construction and land-shaping work (see Chapter 4) – Check slug and snail population (a continuing task)

Early to mid-spring
Prune old fronds – Plant new specimens – Divide those plants which need propagating – Mulch

Late spring/early summer
Continue mulching if not complete – Enjoy new growth

High summer to early autumn
Harvest and sow ripe spores – Propagate new young stock of *Polystichum setiferum* varieties – Visit fern nurseries, exhibits and gardens to select further additions to collection

Late summer through autumn
Grow on new young plants from spores, bulbils etc.

Late autumn and winter
Tidy ferns of loose, slug-friendly detritus – Drop hints to friends and relations about new ferns and books you would be pleased to receive!

Fresh fronds of *Polypodium vulgare* produced in summer now in association with the autumn hardy cyclamen, *C. hederifolium*.

CHAPTER 7

Selected Alphabetical List of Fern Species and Cultivars

Gardeners know that botanists like playing games. It is a good day if between breakfast and suppertime some botanist somewhere has not changed the name of one or more ferns. Often this takes the form of shuttling a species back and forward between two genera, as is the case with the hart's tongue fern which never knows whether it is in bed with the *Asplenium* or *Phyllitis* family. Do not despair. I try to give the commonest synonyms, but have taken *The Encyclopaedia of Ferns* by David L. Jones as the authority to follow. If you are in difficulty you may find a current edition of *The Plant Finder* useful to establish the names currently in use in Britain for kinds offered for sale. You will find that it does not agree in all cases with the names used in this book but it does give synonyms so that it is easy to track down the plant you are interested in.

Some of the information is compressed to save space and repetition. For each entry the botanical name is given first, followed by the common name (not necessarily universally used) and then an indication of natural distribution (unless a nursery-selected or raised cultivar). Also listed are:

F Frond length. The range of length given is due to natural variation within species but even more as a result of habitat conditions.

acid/alkaline Most ferns are tolerant of a range of pH values and will be very happy with neutral soil, but a preference for acid or alkaline soils is shown. Similarly, it is assumed that all ferns will flourish in moist conditions, so **dry** indicates a fern capable of growing in less moist conditions than most; **wet** a preference for extremely damp soil.

ADIANTUM

Adiantum pedatum AMERICAN MAIDENHAIR
N. America, N. India, Japan
F 30–50 cm (12–20 in); acid; deciduous
This is a variable, distinct and very attractive species which is well worth having in every collection. Creeping dark wiry rhizomes produce many erect thread-thin but strong stems, in the usual forms some 30 cm (12 in) or so high. The frond blades are displayed almost horizontally as a series of opposite fan-like oblong blades. Colour is a rich matt green. The overall blade length will be around 10 cm (4 in). It does best in cool shaded spots. Plants increase steadily in size in humus-rich soils. All forms are attractive.
***A.p.* 'Aleuticum'** A Canadian form, with frond blades usually pointing more upwards. It is much dwarfer, at only 10–15 cm (4–6 in), a hummock of pale green with a hazy bloom finish.

Adiantum × tracyi
N. America
F 40–60 cm (16–24 in); acid; deciduous
Pleasing cold-resistant sterile hybrid between *A. pedatum* and *A. jordanii* (the Californian maidenhair), which has appeared sporadically in the wild. Its fronds are more heavily divided than *A. pedatum*, being 2–3 pinnate.

Adiantum venustum   EVERGREEN MAIDENHAIR
N. India, Canada
F 25–75 cm (10–30 in); acid; evergreen
This is a reliable strong plant with wide, more or less triangular frond blades some 12–30 cm (5–12 in) long and divided 3–4 pinnate. Creeping roots will support a wide plant that is very lovely in spring with pale green crosiers and fronds, these taking on a distinct bluish shade with maturity.

ASPLENIUM

Asplenium adiantum-nigrum   BLACK SPLEENWORT
Europe inc. Britain, Africa, Asia, N. America
F 12–40 cm (5–16 in); alkaline/dry; evergreen
This globe-trotting little species is often found growing on walls, often in old mortar. It is a proper miniaturized fern, with long triangular frond blades 2–3 pinnate, distinctively leathery-textured and of a well-polished dark green. It is more tolerant of sun than most and looks well in the rock or sink garden in a well-drained spot.

Asplenium ceterach **(syn. *Ceterach officinarum*)**
RUSTY-BACK FERN
Europe inc. Britain, Africa, India
F 5–15 cm (2–6 in); alkaline/dry; evergreen
This is another of the delightful little plants that can colonize an old wall, making free with the mortar and being able to withstand long periods of drought. It behaves rather like the so-called resurrection ferns in that the fronds can curl up and look dead but be quickly unfurled and prettily displayed with a shower of rain. Thick-textured, paired pinnae are somewhat square with the corners rounded off, their undersides thickly covered with silvery brown scales. This useful little fern can be grown in a corner of the rock garden, on walls, or in containerized miniature gardens.

Asplenium × hybridum
Mediterranean
F 5–15 cm (2–6 in); acid/dry; evergreen
A series of pinnatifid fertile hybrids between *A. ceterach* and *A. sagittatum*, a somewhat larger species.

Asplenium ruta-muraria   WALL RUE or WALL
SPLEENWORT
Europe inc. Britain, Asia, N. America
F 5–10 cm (2–4 in); alkaline/dry; evergreen
More often seen on walls than the rock crevices which are its natural habitat. A very dark little plant with small thick blades of a few pinnae and wiry stems. Best grown on walls, being introduced as spores or tiny plants raised from spores, as it dislikes the root disturbance likely to be encountered with pot culture.

Asplenium scolopendrium **(syn. *Phyllitis scolopendrium*)**   HART'S TONGUE
Europe inc. Britain, Asia, N. America
F 23–60 cm (9–24 in); alkaline; evergreen
The undivided fronds of this famliar wild plant are especially lovely when new, but they can maintain a very dressy appearance for months and, in a spot free of buffeting wind, can be one of the best kinds through the winter months. For this reason it is worth growing some of the better mutant forms – but do not forgo the type.
***A.s.* 'Capitatum'**   Heavy crests at the frond ends.
***A.s.* 'Crispum'**   A sterile form, with the margins beautifully crimped into a ruff. Should be in every collection.
***A.s.* 'Crispum Golden Queen'**   Distinguished by its frilled fronds and glowing golden-green colour.
***A.s.* 'Digitatum'**   Very different from the type, with very divided cristate fronds ending with wide flat crests. the whole is likened by some to the fingers of a hand.

***Adiantum pedatum*, the very distinct fern with fronds held almost horizontally on thread-like wiry stems, here in company with *Lonicera standishii* and *Cotoneaster horizontalis*.**

**The silver birch has the hart's tongue fern at its base and the
male ferns as neighbours.**

A.s. 'Laceratum' As its name implies, has fronds with cut margins.

A.s. 'Marginatum' Distinctly narrower fronds than type, and these deeply cut.

A.s. 'Marginatum Irregulare' A form in which the margins are more randomly lobed and cut.

A.s. 'Sagittatum' As the name suggests, the blades are shaped like arrow heads, the bases being deeply lobed to give this effect.

Asplenium trichomanes   COMMON or MAIDENHAIR SPLEENWORT
Worldwide
F 10–40 cm (4–16 in); alkaline; evergreen
A pretty little fern to be found growing happily on walls, especially in old mortar with some lime. The largest colony I know is in such a wall facing west, but the plants will grow in any exposure. The plants make a neat rosette of many dark stemmed fronds, each carrying perhaps over thirty pairs of matched pinnae. Purple-black stems contrast with the shining bright green of the oval pinnae. There is a subspecies, *A.t.* ssp. *trichomanes* which is similar but is a lime-hater.

A.t. 'Cristatum' This is a fertile form that first appeared in Britain in which each pinna is much divided into crests.

Asplenium viride   GREEN or GREEN-RIBBED SPLEENWORT
Europe inc. Britain, Asia, N. America
F 10–15 cm (4–6 in); alkaline; evergreen
Another pretty miniature, rather like the last species but more usually found on moist rock surfaces rather than walls. It differs also by having green stems, rachis, palmate veining and lightly serrated margins. These serrations are rounded and the colour is a lighter green. It grows well in a rock garden corner or in pots with some lime in the soil.

ATHYRIUM

Athyrium deltoidofrons
China, Korea, Japan
F 25–50 cm (10–20 in); acid; deciduous
Attractive bipinnate yellow-green triangular fronds that look well against neighbouring darker kinds. Best in not too deep shade.

Athyrium distentifolium (syn. A. alpestre) ALPINE LADY FERN
Europe inc. Britain, Iceland, N. America
F 25–50 cm (10–20 in); acid; deciduous
Delicately posed, erect, pale green fronds are triangular in outline, similar to the lady fern but usually smaller with proportionately broader pinnae. Creeping rhizomes can make pleasing plants with rounded rosettes of fronds.

Athyrium filix-femina   LADY FERN
Europe inc. Britain, India, China, Japan, N. and S. America
F 50–150 cm (20–60 in); acid; deciduous
This widespread popular fern grows best in deep loamy humus-rich soils in shade or semi-shade. It is one of the most lively mutators, at one time having over 300 named forms. The type is graceful, usually bipinnate, with long lacy fronds of light green, though some forms are darker.

A.f-f. 'Congestum' Dwarf with well-formed narrowly pointed fronds. Around 15 cm (6 ins) high. The variety 'Congestion Minus' is a diminutive, neat fern with precise, well-cut fronds in attractive rosettes.

A.f-f. 'Congestum Cristatum' Little fern with intricately cut, densely packed fronds with terminal crests.

A.f-f. Cristatum group A series of fertile plants, the pinnae of which have crests displayed flat like fans all along the margins and at the end of each frond. The series is variable; it is wise to see the plant you are buying, some are considerably more ornate than others. 50–90 cm (20–36 in).

A.f-f. 'Fieldii' An unusual form with long narrow fronds with short pinnae arranged in pairs and so forming crosses with their opposite pairs. A curious effect on fronds that can be 90 cm (36 in) long.

A.f-f. 'Frizelliae' The tatting fern. The slender rachis appears to be threaded with a series of paired beads, the pinnae being reduced to flattish rich green balls. 25–50 cm (10–20 in). There are also variants, such as 'Frizelliae Capitatum' and 'Frizelliae Cristatum' where the frond ends have severally branched crests.

A.f-f. 'Glomeratum' A form with narrow fronds with both pinnae and ends crested.

A.f-f. 'Minutissimum' A very pretty light green fertile mutant, with many well-furnished long, triangular, bipinnate fronds. These may measure 12–20 cm (5–8 in) long. Clumps look very pleasing.

A.f-f. Plumosum group A series of plants 20–40 cm (8–16 in) tall, having light green fronds pleasingly divided perhaps three or four times pinnate. The best forms are wonderfully intricate and pure magic when grown in a sheltered shaded or semi-shaded spot. Fronds float like feathers.

A.f-f. 'Victoriae' Strong plant but most interestingly styled in delicate filigree parts. Fronds end in tassles and all the pinnae and their divisions are arranged in pairs at right angles to each other, forming delightfully tasselled crosses.

Athyrium frangulum
Japan
F 12–40 cm (5–16 in); acid; deciduous
A pretty, lightly coloured kind with the rachis a reddish purple. Double or triple pinnate arrangement of widely triangular fronds very well displayed in a crowded arrangement. Very distinctive between rocks.

Athyrium niponicum pictum   JAPANESE PAINTED FERN
Japan, Korea, China
F 40–60 cm (16–24 in); acid; deciduous
This is a lovely fern for a sheltered spot, the name gives a clue to its attraction. Like the last species this is broadly triangular with a pointed frond end. It is usually bipinnate but can be tripinnate. To get the best colouring in the young fronds the plants want to be in shade but with plenty of light, when the rachis and pinnae ribs are a rich burgundy while the soft grey green of the blade can be suffused with red and blue shades merging to green at the margins. Mature fronds are still colourful, though darker, and make patterns of colour, tone and form with the brighter colours of the younger ones.

Athyrium pycnocarpum   AMERICAN GLADE FERN
N. America
F 50–120 cm (20–48 in); acid; deciduous
Wide rosettes of spreading bold fronds, light green in youth but becoming darker and turning warm buff before being discarded. Protect young growth from slugs etc.

BLECHNUM

Blechnum penna-marina   ALPINE WATER FERN
New Zealand, Australia, S. America
F 15–30 cm (6–12 in); acid/wet; evergreen
Makes a good ground-cover plant, rapidly colonizing moist open soils rich in humus. Rather like *B. spicant* but a somewhat smaller, more social spreading plant with many narrow single pinnate well-furnished fronds making dense cover. It will withstand quite a lot of sunshine provided the roots are moist. Will respond well to feeding. There is a smaller subspecies of similar character, *B.p-m* ssp. *alpina*, the pinnae neatly jostling each other along the rachis.

Ferns happy in a garden setting. Here are male ferns,
Dryopteris filix-mas, at Longstock Hampshire, UK.

Small pond planted around with grasses and ferns in half shade, a natural and pleasing combination that does well in even more difficult very shady areas.

Blechnum spicant   HARD FERN
Europe inc. Britain, N. America
F 25–60 cm (10–24 in); acid; evergreen
Sterile fronds have an outline shaped like a spearhead, four or five times longer than broad. These spread out more or less horizontally, being neatly and singly pinnate. Pinnae are close to each other down to the rootstock. The fertile fronds are dissimilar; they are upright and have narrow well-separated pinnae looking like a sparse comb. Colour overall is a rich light green. There are a number of crested mutants and ones with pinnae variously cut.

Blechnum vulcanicum   WEDGE WATER FERN
Australia, New Zealand
F 12–40 cm (5–16 in); acid/wet; evergreen
Typical *Blechnum*, with singly pinnate fronds like the hard fern but with the pinnae distinctly more pointed, fertile ones being very much narrower, and all arranged with stripe (stalk) almost as long as blade on sterile fronds and possible longer on fertile ones. Needs moisture, shade and no disturbance.

CETARACH. See *Asplenium cetarach*

CRYPTOGRAMMA

Cryptogramma crispa   PARSLEY FERN
Europe, Asia Minor, Afghanistan
F 5–25 cm (2–10 in); acid; deciduous
A small fern that can sometimes be found growing wild in scree conditions. Not the easiest of garden plants and any lime is poison to it. The small fronds look not unlike parsley, but only appear in early summer and die away for the winter.

CYRTOMIUM (syn. PHANEROPHLEBIA)

Cyrtomium falcatum   JAPANESE HOLLY FERN
Japan, Korea, China
F 25–50 cm (10–20 in); acid/alkaline; evergreen

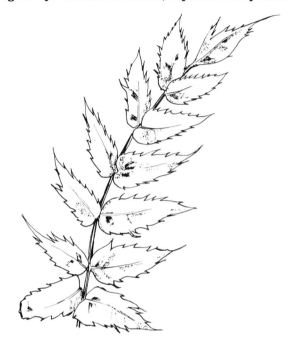

Fig. 16 *Cyrtomium falcatum*, Japanese holly fern.

A popular kind, sensibly named as the dark green, shiny, thick-textured fronds look very much like holly leaves but with rather smaller, more numerous serrations (Fig. 16). Spreading display manner. Very adaptable as far as soils and positions are concerned and able to form very persistent, spreading colonies in healthy soils. Various forms have been selected.
***C.f.* 'Butterfield'** Looking more prickly than the species, with teeth slenderly pointed.
***C.f.* 'Mayi' ('Cristata')** Unusual, with pinnae and frond ends crested; fronds can also be divided.
***C.f.* 'Rochfordianum'** Probably the most widespread. Good dark form with well-defined holly serrations. Makes a fine cool greenhouse plant.

Cyrtomium fortunei
Japan, Korea, China
F 20–40 cm (8–16 in); acid; evergreen and deciduous
Like *C. falcatum* but without serrations, having narrower longer pinnae and held much more upright. Shiny tough texture and rich green in colour.

Cyrtomium lonchitoida
Japan, Korea, China
F 50–90 cm (29–36 in); acid; evergreen and deciduous
Impressive, long narrow oblong fronds with wide diamond-shaped pinnae in bright light green. It has a smoothly polished dressy appearance, with the pinnae ends curved.

CYSTOPTERIS

Cystopteris bulbifera   BERRY BLADDER FERN
N. America
F 30–75 cm (12–30 in); alkaline; deciduous
Bipinnate fronds tend to hang or fall from its preferred site, any semi-shaded bank or rock side with plenty of moisture and soil that is limy. Many bulbils are produced on the undersides of the fronds and these fall to the ground to form new plants.

Cystopteris fragilis   BRITTLE BLADDER FERN
Almost worldwide
F 10–30 cm (4–12 in); deciduous
A dwarf species that is widespread on rocky mountainsides. The fragile fronds are easily broken or spoilt and perish with colder weather. It enjoys shade and moisture in rocky spot or stony soil.

DAVALLIA

Davallia marieseii   HARE'S FOOT FERN
Japan, Korea
F 15–30 cm (6–12 in); acid; deciduous
Unusual and popular species that is hardy in milder regions. In harder areas it makes a fine cool house

plant. Has long been used as a pot plant or in hanging baskets as the furry creeping rhizomes will wander at will or can be trained. At intervals it produces very delicate lacy triangular-bladed fronds, two, three or four times pinnate. *D.m. stenolepis* is a stronger version, the scaly rhizomes being almost white.

DRYOPTERIS

Dryopteris aemula   HAY-SCENTED BUCKLER FERN
Europe inc. Britain
F 25–60 cm (10–24 in); acid; deciduous
A pretty fern with bi- and often partially tripinnate triangular fronds that arch outwards in a graceful manner. The common name is justified by the scent given off by a series of glands on the underside of the fronds. The stalks, approximately half the length of the fronds, shining rich green with the strong stems a purple-black contrasting with the fawn of the scales. It is found in moist, semi-shaded positions in the wild and likes similar spots in the garden.

Dryopteris affinis (syn. D. pseudomas)
SCALY MALE FERN
Europe inc. Britain, S. W. Asia
F 50–150 cm (20–60 in); acid; deciduous
Young fronds are a yellowish green, becoming darker, as they age. Pinnate frond blades are long, relatively narrow and almost equally wide down their length. Pinnae are deeply lobed. It has given rise to some very fine garden plants.
***D.a.* 'Cristata Angustata'** 40–60 cm (16–24 in). A lighter-weight appearance and not so strong as the next variety. Pinnae joined and precisely crested.
***D.a.* 'Cristata The King'** 50–90 cm (20–36 in). Bold and outstandingly attractive. The parallel-sided rich green, firm-textured fronds are displayed in a very even pattern, quite upright but arching outwards and precisely and boldly crested at every pinna and frond

73

**An effective piece of planting design with contrasting foliage
of lady fern, *Athyrium filix-femina*, broad-leaved hostas and
erect swords of iris.**

Collection of ferns in Shropshire garden. Forms of ground-covering *Polypodium vulgare* and an upright *Dryopteris filix-mas* are prominent.

end. Should be in every collection. Strong plant that divides easily.

D.a. 'Grandiceps' With tassellated crests to frond ends.

D.a. 'Grandiceps Askew' 45–60 cm (18–24 in). Strong plant with notably divided and large terminal crests. Very easy and very impressive after a season or so if allowed space.

D.a. 'Grandiceps Harvey' 40–60 cm (16–24 in). Strong-growing kind with good terminal crests, rather narrower frond blades.

D.a. 'Ramosissima' 30–50 cm (12–20 in). The fronds break into many branches, each ending with large crests.

D.a. 'Tavelii' (syn. D.a. 'Stablerii') 45–60 cm (18–24 in). A rich, deep green, erect form with fairly narrow but well-furnished bipinnate blades, the pinnae being neatly indented and broad so that they almost overlap. The central scaly rootstock base makes a telling contrast in orange.

Dryopteris atrata (syn. D. cycadina?) SHAGGY SHIELD FERN
India, Thailand, China, Japan
F 50–90 cm (20–36 in); wet; deciduous
Can be a most impressive, distinct fern, with the stripe and underside of the rachis clothed with black scales. With stems half the length of the arching fronds the whole looks very graceful, the pinnae being from 10 cm (4 in) to possibly twice this length and deeply serrated.

Dryopteris carthusiana NARROW or PRICKLY BUCKLER FERN
Europe inc. Britain, N. America
F 30–120 cm (12–48 in); acid/alkaline; evergreen and deciduous
Perhaps best left in the wild as it can spread itself around too freely. Bipinnate with fronds a broad pointed lance shape and measuring up to 1–1.2 m (3–4 ft) long, one third of which is the stalk.

Dryopteris clintoniana
N. America
F 50–100 cm (20–40 in); acid/wet; evergreen
Established as a species, but thought to have arisen as a hybrid between *D. cristata* and *D. goldieana*. Can make an impressive large plant in a wet position, with spreading broad fronds either singly or doubly pinnate.

Dryopteris cristata CRESTED BUCKLER or SHIELD FERN
Europe, inc. Britain, Siberia, Japan, N. America
F 50–100 cm (20–40 in); acid/wet; evergreen and deciduous
Plants grow easily in moist shady areas to form spreading rosettes of singly pinnate fronds, these contrasting with the less well-furnished upright fertile fronds.

Dryopteris cycodina. See **D. atrata**

Dryopteris dilatata BROAD BUCKLER FERN
Europe inc. Britain, N. & S. America, Greenland, Japan
F 30–150 cm (12–60 in); acid/alkaline; deciduous
A strong-growing species particularly good in moist situations. It will grow well in soils with some lime if given a generous humus ration. It makes broad triangular fronds of rich green arranged as bi- or tripinnate blades that are widespreading and held by rich green stems. A good specimen which has got well established in deep leaf-mould may reach a very spectacular 1.2–1.5 m (4–5 ft); in less favoured spots fronds may be down to as little as 30 cm (12 in). Old plants will form a thick rootstock, sometimes like a mini-trunk.

D.d. 'Grandiceps' 50–90 cm (20–36 in). A mass of tassels in a thick bunch formed by crested ends of fronds, but with crests also on the flat pinnae. Impressive when settled in, perhaps beginning to come to its best in its second or third year.

D.d. 'Lepidota' The finely cut segments give it an airy look.

D.d. 'Lepidota Cristata' 30–60 cm (12–24 in). Makes the most of the finely cut appearance with crested pinnae and branching fronds.

Dryopteris erythrosora   AUTUMN FERN
China, Korea, Japan
F 20–50 cm (8–20 in); acid/alkaline; deciduous
Probably one of the kinds that should be included in the first six for a beginner. Called the autumn fern because of the beautiful colours of the young fronds, this is a species that grows well in almost any soil so long as it is well drained. While it is grown in positions from deep shade to fairly sunny, the plants are probably at their best in moist soil in semi-shade. Pointed, broad triangular fronds regularly furnished down to the base are arranged as a loose-spreading rosette. The blades are polished and when newly unfurled can be very rich shades of coppery gold, orange or red. This colouring lasts for a good number of weeks before giving way to the rich green of maturity. As plants usually continue to produce new fronds through the main growing months there is usually a pleasing medley of colours to enjoy, though the plant would still be worth growing if it were a very standard green.

Dryopteris filix-mas   MALE FERN
Europe inc. Britain, Asia, N. America
F 50–150 cm (20–60 in); acid/alkaline; deciduous
A strong-growing species, and a familiar wild fern in many areas. By no means unspectacular when growing well and shining in the fresh lighter greens of the newer fronds and the darker shades of adulthood. Fronds have pinnae from close to the rootstock and

are held at an angle not too far from the vertical so that a strong plant makes a significant impression. The orange-scaled curled crosiers unfolding is one of the ever-fresh pleasures of springtime. The type may be thought too bold or, dare one say it, too well-known for the smaller garden, but there are many delightful selections that can be really very distinct from mother! If possible see the plant you purchase so that you get a good example.

D.f-m. 'Crispa' Usually only about 30 cm (12 in) high. Very pleasing as a compact sturdy plant, with well-crested, tightly packed fronds.

D.f-m. 'Crispa Cristata' 30–40 cm (12–16 in). A good strong plant with the rich green fronds precisely crested along the pinnae ends and at the apex.

D.f-m. 'Cristata' 50–120 cm (20–48 in). (Be careful with the names as this is a much larger plant than the last.) Pinnae and frond ends neatly crested – almost like parsley.

D.f-m. 'Cristata Jackson' 60–90 cm (24–36 in). A particularly good selection with more curly crests to pinnae and frond ends.

D.f-m. 'Cristata Martindale' 40–45 cm (16–18 in). Exceptionally effective, with the pinnae ends very neatly crested and leading to the wide fish-tailed crested end of the frond. Strong plant.

D.f-m. 'Depauperata' 40–60 cm (16–24 in). Dark fronds with narrower pinnae, the segments more or less fused together. Polished appearance.

D.f-m. 'Grandiceps Wills' 60–90 cm (24–36 in). Grows with great vigour to make a wide plant of several crowns, each donating tall, shining green fronds boldly crested along their margins and ends.

D.f-m. 'Mapplebeck' 60–90 cm (24–36 in). A strong kind with wide fronds and pinnae. Pinnae finished with widely divided crests, while most fronds finish with several branches that are also crested. Each rachis is pleasingly clothed with orangey scales.

77

**Hart's tongue fern seen growing in a collection of plants as
effective for their foliage as for flowers.**

One of the attractive mutant cultivars of the evergreen hart's tongue fern, *Asplenium scolopendrium* 'Marginatum-contractum'.

D.f-m. 'Polydactyla' 30–50 cm (12–20 in). Narrower, shorter fronds than type and with fussy, curly, intricate crests at pinna and frond ends.

D.f-m. 'Polydactyla Dadds' 30–45 cm (12–18 in). In this clone the fronds are less crowded and the cresting flatter, more spreading and perhaps more refined.

Dryopteris goldiana   GIANT WOOD FERN
N. America
F 60–120 cm (24–48 in); acid; deciduous
The large fronds look well in moist shady spot. Young fronds are covered with white and fawn scales, which make it look quite distinct.

Dryopteris marginalis   MARGINAL SHIELD FERN
N. America
F 25–60 cm (10–24 in); acid/alkaline; deduous
Singly or doubly pinnate, with tough textured dark blue-green fronds in tufts. Grows in humus-rich shade.

Dryopteris oreades   MOUNTAIN MALE FERN
Europe
F 25–60 cm (10–24 in); acid/alkaline; deciduous
Singly pinnate, narrow, light green fronds in tufts. Found growing among rocks in European mountain ranges.

Dryopteris parallelogramma. See **D. wallichiana**

Dryopteris phegopteris. See **Phegopteris connectilis**

Dryopteris pseudo-mas. See **D. affinis**

Dryopteris sieboldii
China, Japan
F 15–40 cm (6–16 in); acid; deciduous
Little plant with each frond having a few large tough pinnae which droop. An unusual non-rampant character plant.

Dryopteris thelypteris. See **Thelypteris palustris**

Dryopteris wallichiana (syn. parallelogramma)
India, China, Japan, N. and C. America, Africa
F 50–100 cm (20–40 in); acid/alkaline; deciduous
As it grows this species forms a tough, almost trunk-like rootstock from which a fountain of fronds appear, shining light gold and yellowy greens in their energetic spring flush, colouring that is highlighted by black rachis. Plant in loamy soil (does not mind lime) in a shady position.

GYMNOCARPIUM

Gymnocarpium dryopteris   OAK FERN
Europe inc. Britain, India, China, Japan, N. America
F 15–30 cm (6–12 in); acid; evergreen and deciduous
Thin underground stems will support a clump of widely spaced fronds, their broadly triangular shape being made up by the three triangular branched blades of the fronds. The colour is pale green. There is a form called *G.d.* 'Plumosum' which is finely cut to give an even lighter, more feathery feel, the broader pinnules tending to overlap. Plants should be grown in open, humus-rich soil that does not dry out, perhaps in a shaded part of a rock bed or towards the front of the fernery.

Gymnocarpium robertianum   LIMESTONE OAK FERN
Europe, N. America
F 15–45 cm (6–18 in); alkaline; deciduous
Attractive small creeping fern with very pleasing tripinnate fronds sent up at intervals from the widespreading rootstock. A pretty ground-cover plant for shady spots with lime in soil.

MATTEUCCIA

Matteuccia orientalis
China, Korea, Japan
F 30–90 cm (12–36 in); acid; deciduous
Similar to the next species but smaller.

Matteuccia struthiopteris OSTRICH FEATHER or SHUTTLECOCK FERN
China, Japan, N. America, introduced (?) Europe
F 50–150 cm (20–60 in); acid; deciduous
One of the easiest and most effective ferns grown in neutral or somewhat acid soils, with some shade and reasonable moisture. Erect fronds form a tall vase or shuttlecock shape, the precise design of which is a marvel as one looks down. Running rhizomes just below the soil surface are marked at intervals by new smaller fronds that quickly grow to mature size. If the colony gets overcrowded some plants should be removed. Fertile fronds may arise in the centre of the shuttlecock; only a third of the height of the sterile fronds, if that, they are brown and look as if made of plastic.

ONOCLEA

Onoclea sensibilis SENSITIVE or BEAD FERN
N. Asia, N. America
F 25–60 cm (10–24 in); acid to neutral; deciduous
Singly or double pinnate, robust, low fern with crowded triangular, light green fronds. Normal forms are singly pinnate but with pinnae lobed to give a pinnatifid effect. It can be made very happy by waterside where it will run about to form considerable colonies, the fronds often lasting quite late into the end of the year before being seen off by hard frosts. The fertile fronds are quite dissimilar, with spore-bearing sporangia being formed into bunches like so many beads or bunches of small grapes. While some have green stems and rachis, there is a more decorative one with red stems.

OSMUNDA

Osmunda banksiifolia
China, Japan
F 25–90 cm (10–36 in); acid/wet; deciduous

Singly pinnate, light green, thin fronds have lightly lobed segments. It likes shade, humus and acid soil with much water.

Osmunda japonica
Japan, Korea, China, N. India
F 25–90 cm (10–36 in); acid/wet; deciduous
Very similar to royal fern, below, but smaller.

Osmunda regalis ROYAL FERN
Europe inc. Britain, Africa, Asia, N. and S. America
F 60–180 cm (2–6 ft); acid to neutral/wet; deciduous
Probably the most imposing of the hardy ferns, certainly the largest once established in a waterside site. In a sheltered favourable spot a mature specimen can produce fronds that can be between 3 and 4 m (10–12 ft) long, with their blades 1 m (3 ft) across. In a less favoured place the plant can still look impressive even with fronds only 60 cm (2 ft) long.

Old established plants will form large hummocks of woody rootstocks from which arise in spring the new orangey stems with distinct crosiers slowly unfurling. The stout stems are orangey brown in youth but become yellowish later. Doubly pinnate spreading blades are bright light green when young but become darker with maturity. The fertile fronds are sent up erectly and give the effect of a clustered head of some massive dock-like flower, something that has given rise to the false name of the flowering fern. The first frost transforms all into a rusted mass, but the fawny brown winter effect is not without decorative appeal. Everyone will enjoy the royal fern, not all will have the space to house it adequately.
***O.r.* 'Cristata'.** An unusual crested form.

Osmunda spectabilis
F 90–150 cm (36–60 in); acid/wet; deciduous.
A rather more upright grower than *O. regalis*, sometimes reaching 1.5 cm (5 ft). Its fronds are palish green in colour and have slender pinnae.

Dryopteris dilatata, the broad buckler fern, usually
tripinnate and very strong growing. In favourable wet sites
fronds can be 1 m ($3\frac{1}{4}$ ft) long.

83

Dryopteris filix-mas 'Grandiceps Askew'. A selected clone of
the 'Grandiceps' series of the male fern, particularly robust
and distinctly crested.

PHEGOPTERIS

Phegopteris ***connectilis*** **(syn.** ***Thelypteris phegopteris, Dryopteris phegopteris*)** BEECH FERN
Europe inc. Britain, Asia, N. America
F 15–45 cm (6–18 in); acid; deciduous.
With thin creeping rhizomes this species can form loose colonies in its preferred moist mountain streamside or woodland habitats. The frond stems may be twice the length of the singly or doubly pinnate fronds, and the fronds themselves are the traditional long-pointed fern triangular. A diagnostic feature is the way the lowest pair of pinnae, usually well clear of the remainder, turn or curve away from the blade, a habit not echoed by any of the other pairs.

PHYLLITIS. See ***Asplenium scolopendrium***

POLYPODIUM

Polypodium australe SOUTHERN POLYPODY
Europe inc. Britain
F 20–45 cm (8–18 in); acid/alkaline; evergreen and deciduous.
Singly pinnate and similar to the common polypody, *P. vulgare*, it differs in having broader blades, widest at the second, third, or fourth pair of pinnae, and usually with pinnae gently but more serrated than in the common polypody. Leaf texture is also less tough. It grows easily in semi-shade, given a loamy soil with plenty of humus. New fronds do not appear until the summer and autumn.
***P. a.* 'Cambricum'** An attractive form originally found near Powis Castle in Wales, growing on rocks in a wood, though it has been recorded at other sites in the principality. The pinnae are broader and deeply lobed and divided, tending to overlap each other.
***P. a.* 'Pulcherrimum'** In this fertile form the divisions of the pinnae usually extend right up to the midribs.

Polypodium scouleri LEATHERY POLYPODY
N. America
F 20–45 cm (8–19 in); acid; deciduous.
Polished green tough blades with the divisions reaching about two-thirds the way to the midribs. This is a slow growing plant that needs good drainage, shade and to be allowed to get on in its own time.

Polypodium vulgare COMMON POLYPODY
Europe inc. Britain, Africa, China, Japan, N. America.
F 10–45 cm (4–18 in); acid/alkaline; evergreen and deciduous.
Stalks are about a third of the full frond lengths and arise from creeping rhizomes. In the longer fronds the

Fig. 17 ***Polypodium vulgare*, common polypody.**

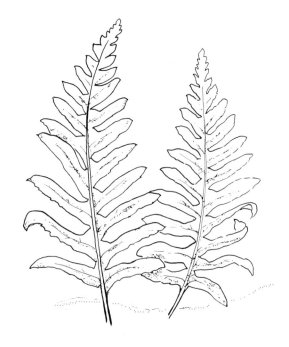

outline is of an almost parallel-sided, singly pinnate leaf a quarter wide as long, perhaps like a two-sided comb. Fronds end with a single long, blunted-ended pinna. New growth starts late in the year. While it appears to grow in a variety of soils, it certainly seems to enjoy gritty rock soils.

P.v. 'Bifidum' In this form the lower pairs of pinnae are clearly lobed.

P.v. 'Bifidum Cristatum' A form with pinnae lobed to more than half their depth and the fronds ending with a wide crest.

P.v. 'Cornubiense' A schizophrenic fern! Apparently at random it produces three different frond forms. Firstly they are as the type, secondly ones that are filigree with divisions tri- or even quadripinnate with very thin segments, and thirdly a rather less sophisticated bolder form of this last. It makes an interesting little spreading plant to have at the front of the fernery and here you may even find a single frond trying to adopt all three forms, poor mixed-up entity!

P.v. 'Cristatum' This is the standard article, but with pinnae and frond ends crested.

P.v. 'Interjectum' A form with wider blades and with the basal and perhaps the next pair of pinnae turned sharply inwards.

P.v. 'Longicaudatum' As type but with the terminal segment of each frond palely coloured and pulled out to a very long point.

P.v. 'Racemosum' Fronds are decoratively forked.

P.v. 'Racemosum Hillman' Fronds forked and sometimes crested.

POLYSTICHUM

Polystichum acrostichoides CHRISTMAS FERN
N. America.
F 25–90 cm (10–36 in); acid; evergreen and deciduous.
Attractive in a shady moist spot, especially so in the first flush of youth when the fronds are lit up with a silvery finish. Bold pinnae are rich green and singly pinnate, attractive enough to be sold sometimes as cut foliage.

P.a. 'Crispum' Margins of fronds decorated in a much-curled, attractively fussy finish.

P.a. 'Incisum' While singly pinnate, the pinnae are very deeply cut.

Polystichum aculeatum HARD or PRICKLY SHIELD FERN
Europe inc. Britain, N. India
F 50–120 cm (20–48 in); alkaline; evergreen.
A striking plant in the wild or in the garden. Usually found in woodland or hedgerow, it forms a round clump of fronds, usually 60–90 cm (2–3 ft) long and in maturity a rich dark green. It normally manages to keep its fronds intact through the winter to make a fine contrast to the new light green, unfurling, drooping crosiers that curl over backwards, unlike the conformist majority. Singly or doubly pinnate, the tough lance-shaped pinnae are closely packed together and are deeply incised at their ends giving them a spiky or prickly appearance – hence the common names.

P.a. 'Acutilobum' With narrower, very pointed pinnae.

P.a. 'Cambricum' Segments are egg or sickle shaped and boldly toothed.

P.a. 'Pulcherrimum' Finely drawn kind with lacy fronds with divided, fanned ends.

P.a. 'Pulcherrimum Gracillimum' One of the wonders of the family, the fronds intricately divided into gossamer-thin segments that seem to float in the air. Much to be desired, but a scarce kind that is sterile.

Polystichum andersonii ANDERSON'S HOLLY FERN
N. America
F 25–100 cm (10–40 in); wet; evergreen.
An attractive double pinnate species with hardy, textured holly-like fronds being unusual and generous

**The ostrich feather fern, *Matteuccia struthiopteris*, showing
how it can colonize a site. In a damp spot it can be one of the
easiest and most effective of deciduous ferns.**

87

Polystichum polyblepharum is a very hardy fern from China
and Japan, with tough, textured fronds. The adult rich green
is preceded by the very scaly new crosiers.

in ending with a useful vegetative bulbil. Easy, given moisture and shade.

Polystichum braunii   HOLLY FERN
Europe, China, Japan, N. America.
F 25–100 cm (10–40 in); acid; evergreen and deciduous.
Another bipinnate species that mimics holly. This one is delightful in spring with the new fronds a piece of shimmering silvery magic sculpture. It likes moisture, shade and an open soil, preferably slightly acid.

Polystichum cystostegia
New Zealand
F 10–25 cm (4–10 in); acid/alkaline; evergreen.
A little mountain fern with neat bipinnate fronds made more decorative with orangey brown scales on stems and rachides.

Polystichum imbricans (syn. P. munitum imbricans)
N. America
F 25–60 cm (10–24 in); acid and alkaline; evergreen and deciduous.
Spear-shaped fronds clothed to the base with crowded overlapping pinnae in full rich green.

Polystichum munitum   SWORD FERN
N. America
F 25–100 cm (10–40 in); acid; evergreen and deciduous.
Long, singly pinnate fronds are well-furnished to their bases and basically parallel-sided but tapering to a sword-point finish. Neatly arranged, pointed pinnae are precisely lobed. Good mid-green colour.

Polystichum polyblepharum
China, Korea, Japan
F 50–120 cm (20–48 in); acid; evergreen and deciduous.

Easy in shade with plenty of humus when it will form a rosette of tough, shining fronds either singly or doubly pinnate. Fronds are a dark colour though young ones are paler, scaly and pleasing. Fronds may remain scaly below.

Polystichum retroso-paleaceum
Korea, Japan
F 45–100 cm (18–40 in); acid, evergreen and deciduous.
Can make a spectacular fern in the garden or in a half-tub. A spreading rosette of bipinnate, polished, shining green frond blades with orangey rachides is made the more interesting when the new ones are covered with scales.

Polystichum richardii
New Zealand
F 20–45 cm (8–18 in); acid/alkaline; evergreen and deciduous.
Neat round rosettes of bipinnate, robust fronds are dark green with more than a hint of blue. In shade or semi-shade in open soils it can look neat and effective, a contrast to some paler kinds or to rocks.

Polystichum setiferum   SOFT SHIELD FERN
Europe inc. Britain
F 50–150 cm (20–60 in); acid/alkaline; evergreen and deciduous.
A height of 150 cm (5 ft) is possible but is rarely reached – in the wild 60 cm (2 ft) would be more normal and garden forms are usually less tall. The habit of the plants is spreading with elegant bi- or tripinnate long fronds reaching sideways to display the soft velvety texture, a feeling achieved by the very great number of pinnae, their veining, serration and precise positioning. The soft colouring helps the overall velvety look. In spring the new fronds are a picture as they uncurl themselves from the swathing orangey scales that will remain on the rachis and

around the rootstock. Rounded rosettes of new young plants become more complicated as the specimen ages and forms new crowns.

At all stages this is an attractive plant, the fronds often lasting through the winter looking respectable, but it may be politic to prune away some of the older more weary ones before the new flush appears. Fronds can produce a series of little bulbil plantlets along the rachides at the bases of the pinnae. As these develop, and if you wish to propagate the form, a complete frond can be removed and lowered into a tray of mixed coarse sand and clean humus, kept moist in a polythene cover and the young plants pricked out when they have rooted and started to expand their small fronds.

Over 300 forms have been named in the past.

P.s. **'Acutilobum'** With narrow fronds and very pointed segments. A compact kind.

P.s. **'Congestum'** Miniature fertile form only about 15–18 cm (6–7 in) tall. Erect fronds are bright green and thick with overlapping pinnae, looking most neat and attractive in a rock garden or wherever planted.

P.s. **'Divisilobum'** Gorgeous, with large fronds tri- or quadripinnate delicately cut. Curiously, those on the lower side of the pinnae are longer than those on the upper side. Young fronds as they unfurl are dressed overall with silvery white scales. The fronds reach outwards though often their tips tend to point up. Old established plants in a good spot may be a feature, measuring 1.2–1.5 m (4–5 ft) across.

P.s. **'Divisilobum Iveryanum'** A very classy plant some 15–45 cm (6–18 in) high. Horizontal fronds are intricately divided, with very evenly matched, spreading crests along each margin and finished with an excellent terminal one. Fanciers reckon it one of the finest.

P.s. **'Foliosum'** Very velvety and full with overlapping segments.

P.s. **'Plumosum'** 40–75 cm (16–30 in). Feathery fronds carefully cut into overlapping segments make it a quadripinnate specimen, one of the rare ones to achieve such intricacy. They look mossy soft.

P.s. **'Polydactylum'** Segments end with divided crests.

P.s. **'Pulcherrimum Bevis'** This is a much sought-after cultivar with very precisely and intricately cut fronds held firmly and as if manufactured from some strange metal. As the plant establishes itself it will expand the size of its fronds till they may be over 60 cm (2 ft) long.

P.s. **'Rotundatum'** Unusual form in which the fronds are close to circular.

Polystichum tsus-simense
China, Korea, Japan
F 15–45 cm (6–18 in); acid/alkaline; evergreen and deciduous.

A neat fern with stiff, tough-textured fronds of quite wide, rounded triangular outline, the rather broad pinnae neatly disposed. The rich dark green is suffused with a suggestion of purple when young. Makes tidy, spreading rosettes. Hardy but good in a pot as well.

THELYPTERIS

Thelypteris palustris (syn. *Dryopteris thelypteris*) MARSH FERN
Europe inc. Britain, N. America.
F 75–150 cm (30–60 in); acid/wet; evergreen.

Long, creeping black rhizomes, much branched, give rise to fronds at intervals, these being light green, singly or doubly pinnate with stems as long as the blades. The sterile fronds are produced in the spring, the stouter fertile ones in the early summer. Useful as a colonizer only in very wet acid conditions.

Thelypteris phegopteris. See *Phegopteris connectilis*.

Polystichum setiferum 'Foliosum' is one of the very many cultivars of soft shield fern showing intricately cut lace-like fronds with the soft texture of velvet.

Matteuccia struthiopteris, **the shuttlecock or ostrich feather
fern. The depth of these 'shuttlecocks' is about 75 cm (30 in),
but they can vary from 45–150 cm (18–60 in).**

WOODSIA

Woodsia obtusa   BLUNT-LOBED WOODSIA
N. America
F 15–25 cm (6–10 in); alkaline; deciduous
A small deciduous kind with bipinnate fronds. It does well in shaded well-drained soil, either neutral or somewhat limy.

WOODWARDIA

Woodwardia areolata   CHAIN FERN
N. America
F 50–90 cm (20–36 in); acid/wet; evergreen and deciduous.
Could easily be mistaken for a related *Blechnum* species. The paired pinnae form a series of ladder rungs. The strong, glossy-textured fronds form clumps that grow well in moist acid soils where they stand more sun than most ferns.

Woodwardia fimbriata   GIANT CHAIN FERN
Mexico, N. America.
F 1–2 m (3–6½ ft); acid/alkaline; deciduous.
A robust, large fern with airy, wide triangular bipinnate fronds. Grows best in a moist, shaded spot and there forms upright dark green masses.

Woodwardia orientalis   ORIENTAL CHAIN FERN
N. India, China, Japan
F 1–2.3 m (3–7½ ft); acid, deciduous.
The large, long, widely triangular fronds are tough-textured and a rich green. They arch over and even approach the ground. As fronds age some will give rise to a series of many plantlets sprouting light green fronds, an easy means of increase.

Woodwardia radicans   EUROPEAN CHAIN FERN
Europe, Asia
F 45 cm–2.1 m (1½–7 ft); acid; deciduous.
An impressive long-cultivated, robust fern with arching, shining green fronds. Bipinnate. Needs placing to rear of fernery with room to grow. Substantial bulbils borne at apex of the fronds provide easy method of increase.

Woodwardia virginica
N. America
F 25–60 cm (10–24 in); acid/wet; deciduous.
Creeping rhizomes are often under water and given the right conditions spread quickly. Rich green fronds, 30–45 cm (12–18 in) long, are oblong in shape and bronzed in youth. Plants can look very ornamental in a boggy bit of ground.

Select Bibliography

There are many books on ferns, a large number having been written in Victorian times and in the first decade of this century. Some of these have been reprinted recently and a new flush of books has appeared lately; a selection of each that may be useful to read or consult are listed below.

Druery, C.T. *British Ferns and their Varieties*, Routledge, London (1910).

Hyde, H.A., Wade, A.E., and Harrison, S.G. *Welsh Ferns* (5th edition), National Museum of Wales, Cardiff (1969).

Jones, D.L. *Encyclopaedia of Ferns*, Lothian Publishing Co., Melbourne and British Museum (Natural History), London (1987). Includes a useful full bibliography.

Kaye, R. *Hardy Ferns*, Faber and Faber, London (1968).

Kaye, R. *Ferns* (Wisley Handbook 32), RHS/Cassell, London (1980).

Lovis, J.D. 'Fern Hybridists and Fern Hybridising II: Fern Hybridising at the University of Leeds', *British Fern Gazette*, 10: 13–20 (1968).

Rush, R. *A Guide to Hardy Ferns*, British Pteridological Society, London (1984).

Fern Societies

British Pteridological Society (founded 1891)
A. R. Busby, (Hon. General Secretary), 16 Kirby Corner Rd, Canley, Coventry CV4 8GD.

American Fern Society,
Michael I. Cousens, Faculty of Biology, University of West Florida, Pensacola, Florida 32504
There are up to a dozen other American fern societies based in different states.

Nelson Fern Society
Mrs J. Bonnington, 9 Bay View Road, Atawhai, Nelson, New Zealand.

Fern Society of Victoria,
PO Box 45, Heidelberg, Victoria 3081, Australia.

Fern Society of South Australia,
PO Box 711, GPO, Adelaide, South Australia 5001, Australia.

Tasmanian Fern Society,
Julie Haas, 72 Bush Creek Road, Lenah Valley, Tasmania 7008, Australia.

Japanese Pteridological Society,
Prof. K. Iwatsuki, Dept. of Botany, Faculty of Science, Kyoto University, Kyoto, Japan.

Nippon Fernist Club,
c/o Institute of Forest Botany, Faculty of Agriculture, University of Tokyo, Yayoi-cho, Bunkyo-ku, Tokyo, Japan.

Index

Page numbers in *italic* refer to the photographs

95

ACKNOWLEDGEMENTS

The publishers are grateful to the following for granting permission to reproduce
the following colour photographs: Photos Horticulutral Picture Library (pp. 2, 42,
74 & 78); Michael Jefferson-Brown (pp. 10, 31, 59, 79, 82, 83, 86, 87, 90 & 91). All
the remaining photographs were taken by Bob Challinor.

All the line drawings were drawn by the author.